The Book of
Non-Electric Lighting

Single, duplex, and round-wick kerosene lamps

The Book of Non-Electric Lighting

The Classic Guide to the Safe Use of Candles, Fuel Lamps, Lanterns, Gaslights & Fire-View Stoves

Second Edition

Tim Matson

THE COUNTRYMAN PRESS
Woodstock, Vermont

Library of Congress Cataloging-in-Publication Data
Matson, Tim, 1943–
   The book of non-electric lighting : the classic guide to the safe use of candles,
fuel lamps, lanterns, gaslights & fire-view stoves / Tim Matson.—2nd ed.
      p. cm.
   Rev. ed. of: Alternative light styles, published in 1984.
   Includes bibliographical references and index.
   ISBN 978-0-88150-794-2 (alk. paper)
   1. Light sources. 2. Lighting. 3. Gas-lighting. 4. Candles. 5. Hearths. I.
Matson, Tim, 1943– Alternative light styles. II. Title.
   TH7953.M37 2008
   621.32'3--dc22   2008008967

Deluxe Brass Table Lamp by Aladdin® provided by Lehman's
Mailing address: 289 Kurzen Road N., Dalton, OH 44618
Store address: 4779 Kidron Road, Kidron, OH 44636
888-438-5346, www.lehmans.com

Cover photo by Rick Mastelli/Image & Word
Cover design by Deborah Fillion
Interior photos by the author unless otherwise specified
Page composition by Jacinta Monniere

Published by The Countryman Press, P.O. Box 748, Woodstock, Vermont 05091
Distributed by W.W. Norton & Company, Inc., 500 Fifth Avenue, New York, NY
10110

Printed in the United States of America
10 9 8 7 6 5 4 3 2 1

This book is for my Mom and Dad

Contents

Firelight Revisited
An Introduction to the Second Edition

It gives me great pleasure to reintroduce a book I wrote 25 years ago (hey, I'm still here!), which has been out of print much too long. Admittedly, a book about non-electric lighting didn't exactly rock the casbah during the go-go Reagan years, but what the heck, it was morning in America. Although I think it should have been spelled *mourning.* Anyway, *Alternative Light Styles* was full of useful, sometimes lifesaving information, even if the general public wasn't curious about an occasional (or longer) plunge into darkness. Or perhaps it was the pun-ishing title, which is now updated with the no-nonsense *The Book of Non-Electric Lighting.* It's search engine friendly!

Now here we are in the early years of the 21st century (even though it may feel like it's been going on a lot longer), and you've no doubt heard the Director of Homeland Security warn us all to stash at least three days of household supplies, just in case. (The local fire chief tells me to double that, at least—three years later, some of the surviving homes of Hurricane Katrina are still without electricity!)

The curious thing is that I didn't originally write this book as an emergency preparedness manual, although that may be its primary fate today. Instead, I wrote it mostly for people like myself, who had moved to the country, beyond the electric grid, and needed non-electric lighting. I had lived off-grid for 10 years and knew a lot about non-electric illumination. Candles, kerosene lamps, Aladdin lamps, LP gaslights, a fire-view stove—we had them all and not a single call to the fire department! No electric bills, rolling brownouts, or storm damage blackouts either—not to mention the money saved by buying rural land beyond the electric line. It was all about making that move to the country to live off the land, kiss the suburbs goodbye, and plant the seeds for a more sane and sustainable culture. And a lot of us are still at it, even though it may feel more apocalyptic than utopian.

Fast forward a few more years, and we plugged in. Why? Well, there were kids, my wife and I spent more time working away from home and going out at night, and we didn't feel comfortable mixing teenage baby sitters and kerosene lamps.

Jump ahead another 20 years, and what goes around comes around. I get a phone call from my publisher who's had some inquiries about the light book. One Ohio supplier of implements for rural living, Lehman's, sold the original book and wondered about a revival.

So I make a call. Galen Lehman tells me that he was an early fan of the book, and he's seeing a resurgence in non-electric lighting sales. And why would that be? I ask. Emergency preparedness, off-grid rural homes and cottages, and camping, he says. But what about solar power, windmills, hydro, emergency generators, batteries?

They're all fine, he explains, but not everyone has a backup independent electric system, and batteries can run out. Candles and kerosene lamps are simple and they work. They're convenient and dependable, and people like the old-fashioned aesthetic.

I make a few more calls and do some research. I discover that the Internet is full of sites selling emergency lighting, non-electric fuel lamps and lanterns, LP and natural gas fixtures, outdoor torches, and candles of every stripe—elegant wax candle sculptures, seven day emergency candles, candles to cook on, and perhaps best of all, the organic, non-toxic, renewable resource: naturally sweet-scented beeswax candles. Galen Lehman sends me a wick lamp that burns olive oil. That's a new one for me, but in fact, just about the oldest method of fuel lighting. And talk about a renewable resource.

A few more words about the roots of the firelighting revival. It began with the lead-up to the new millennium—Y2K—and all the gloom and doom prophecies about computer breakdowns, which if you recall promised to lead to total system failure, electricity blackouts, and planes falling out of the sky. But no need to worry if you ordered a year's supply of wheat berries, a grinder, and a whole lot of candles and kerosene lamps! Well, the sky didn't fall, but a year later the twin towers did, and if Y2K didn't do it, 9/11 insured the birth of a robust emergency preparedness industry. Since then we've had self-inflicted climate change or whatever it is (some say it's all the sun's fault!) triggering the town and country-leveling hurricanes Katrina and Rita, unprecedented forest fires wiping out thousands of homes, tornadoes, floods, and an increasing number of blackouts due to electrical overloads, ice storms, and even denial of service to scare up utility rates. According to several suppliers I talked to, every time the TV broadcasts another disaster, emergency lighting sales take off. Need a match?

Then there's the rather impressive pilgrimage to the country, where folks are buying full-time and part-time rural homes, and the electric service is often unreliable or nonexistent. And thus, despite the availability of solar power and fuel-powered electric generators, the demand for candles and fuel lighting does grow.

And why are folks moving? The idyllic rural life, for sure, but there's more. They're also moving for keeps, or buying a country getaway, as an escape from threats of terrorism or infrastructure breakdowns or whatever the latest emergency happens to be.

But cheer up; you don't have to be paranoid to enjoy firelight. The aesthetics of a glowing flame are sufficient. When I wrote the original book, only a handful of woodstove manufacturers were building fire-view doors. Now virtually all stoves and fireplace inserts feature a fire-view. Aladdin lamps are now offered with colorful antique glass shade designs and in heirloom collector editions, as well as the classic homestead models. Candles are a $2-billion annual business in the United States because they're festive, relaxing, spiritually inspiring, and elegant—and great help in a blackout. True, paraffin candles can be a bit sooty, and some people complain that they trigger respiratory problems. Come to think of it, a lot of candles are made in China. Hmmmm . . . I vote for a renaissance of beeswax candles, and a crusade to solve the colony die off problem. Support your local beekeeper!

This new edition of *The Book of Non-Electric Lighting* includes the original and unique material covering all aspects of firelighting. I've updated material where there were changes in products, suppliers, or fuel data over the past two decades. In addition there's an expanded "Sources" section to lead you to some of the best producers and purveyors of firelighting products available in North America. Although this is not a technical manual, *The Book of Non-Electric Lighting* will give you the basic information you need to make intelligent decisions about your lighting options. All information is based on the author's experience, and is not intended to replace manufacturers' instructions. Some of the lamps and stoves described may have been superceded by newer models with different operating procedures. When operating flammable lighting systems, be sure to follow manufacturers' instructions, and never leave a burning candle or lamp unattended.

Nothing could be more natural than a renaissance of firelight. It's the original illuminant, it's back, and I think we'll be seeing a lot more of it in the years to come.

Strafford, Vermont
December 2007

An Explanation

In May 1974, I switched off my electric lights. I cut my electric habit with a vengeance: cold turkey when I was lucky, but mostly pork and beans warmed over a campfire or a candle. By day I built my cabin in the light of the long North Country summer sun, working with a chainsaw and hand tools. At dusk I kindled a fire near the tent. The orange flames threw enough illumination for me to scratch out a few letters and to sharpen the chain saw before the fire died. Sometimes rain sizzled the fire, and I burrowed into the tent. A burning taper cradled in a clay pot beamed spokes of light through holes in the side of the pot. The tent sparkled.

By Halloween I had the cabin closed up. For a brighter night life I brought in a trio of kerosene lamps, which illuminated the early years. Eventually I replaced some of the lamps with brighter liquid propane (LP) mantle lights. (Without a doubt, if you plan to light by fire for primary illumination, LP is tops.) Thus I passed through a condensed evolution of lighting, progressing from Neanderthal campfires to 20th-century mantle lamps. Naturally I considered the next step. That's when I discovered it would cost me close to $3,000 simply to run the electric line up my hill. Then come the bills, the inevitable appliances, the power failures. No, the power line wouldn't do.

I am not alone in this decision. Scattered throughout this small rural town are close to a score of families living year-round without commercial, power company electricity; many light primarily with kerosene lamps and LP, a few with photovoltaic, hydro, and windmill power. The locally generated electricity is experimental, erratic, and expensive. Firelight is inexpensive, reliable, and mobile.

Besides cutting the utility bill, those of us outside the main current often find that "non-electric land" is a very good buy. The soil is likely to be richer and the forest thicker. Certainly the price tag will be lower, along with the taxes, not to mention fuel bills. It costs me less than $100 a year to power the lights. But don't get me wrong. With gas-powered lights, stove, and refrigerator, and fire-view wood stoves, I can't exactly call myself a primitive. An energy vegetarian, perhaps.

And this is just the tip of the iceberg. Electric rates nationwide are soaring. An estimated 25 million mantle lamps burn in this country annually, excluding kerosene wick lamps and lanterns. There are year-round lamp keepers, and people who keep firelights for back-up use during power breaks, weekends, or vacations at a country home, and camping, boating, and special occasions. And special occasions may not always be a festive dinner by candle-light. In the summer of 1982, for instance, 30,000 people in Connecticut were cut off for not paying their electric bills.

Nowadays, the Coleman Company makes more than a million lanterns annually. Aladdin is going strong after a century. LP gaslights, which until recently turned up mostly in recreational vehicles and trailers, are now moving into homes and vacation camps. Humphrey Products has manufactured LP gaslights since 1901, when they supplied much of the outdoor lighting in the United States. I once asked Herb Rosenhagen, president of Humphrey, to give me an estimate of the Humphrey lights in operation.

"It would have to be high in the hundreds of thousands," he said. "That's in the United States, Canada, South America, and the Bahamas. You have to remember that these lights last 30 years."

During the development of my firelight system, it occurred to me that it would have been made immensely easier—and safer—with a guidebook. Too often the lamp keeper's craft is won at the sacrifice of broken chimneys, cracked mantles, or kerosene stains.

Worse, an improperly installed or unmonitored lamp can kill you. I had searched for a book about firelight but found only history that stopped short at about 1900 with the inception of electricity. Electric light seems to have blinded many people to the reality that firelight continues to illuminate homes around the world. Three-quarters of the earth's people still light by fire.

It's interesting also to recall that the Welsbach mantle appeared almost simultaneously with Edison's electric bulb. The Welsbach mantle quadrupled the candlepower of the wick lamps and the gaslights of the time and outperformed electric light during the early century. In rural areas, gaslights, Aladdins, and Colemans continued to rule the night as late as the 1950s. In the history of artificial lighting, the reign of electricity is just the blink of an eye. Indeed, the coming of electrification often has been viewed with suspicion.

Clearly, a fresh look at non-electric light is needed. Advertisements and instruction pamphlets for most lamps highlight the positive side of the unit, of course, but often fail to mention the difficulties: the need for adequate ventilation, flare-ups, mantle protection and radiation, proper fueling, and so forth. Many suppliers have had little experience with their products. For instance, one distributor I know recommended lighting LPs from above, a flat-out dangerous procedure.

I also want to scotch the myth of electric efficiency. When I mentioned to a physicist recently that I use gaslight, his fuse seemed to blow.

"Gaslight is 10 times as wasteful as electric light!" He exploded. "Gaslight disappeared for a good reason. It's grossly inefficient!"

Not quite. Most of the electricity produced today is generated from coal, oil, or uranium—all non-renewable and polluting—and about two-thirds of the energy content in these fuels winds up as wasted heat, not electricity. If that's efficient, we need a new definition of the word. Instead, what we really need are new sources of energy. Photovoltaic cells and wind/hydro generators show promise, as does methane. Methane can be piped from deposits in the earth, or better yet, bacteriologically brewed as a form of solar fuel from manure, garbage, sewage, crop residues, and seaweed. It's easy to transport and can be burned directly or used to generate electricity.

"The fuel that most closely approaches the ideal is methane," wrote Barry Commoner in an essay in *The New Yorker* in May 1983. "It burns with the blue flame familiar from the kitchen stove or with the bright yellow flame of the gaslight that once illuminated streets, homes, and shops." Today, the fuel burned in most North American wick and mantle lamps is kerosene, not methane. But as Commoner points out, hundreds of thousands of methane generators provide villages in Asia with fuel for lights, cooking, and some farmers in this country have adopted the technique. It would be simple to convert LP gaslights, for instance, to methane.

For now, firelight seems possessed of a schizophrenic nature. There's a classic aura about it that epitomizes the 19th-century pre-electric era; yet there's a post-industrial, 20th-century survivalist spirit, too. Look at the fuel burning lamp as a museum piece or as a pioneering element in your home. Either way, firelight burns like a torch passed through history, connecting the past—the time we first dared to kindle our own suns—and what's to come.

Candlepower

In the beginning—before chimney lamps or electricity—was the candle. And when the power fails, the candle reappears. It is the one truly independent light: fuel and wick fused into a single element, no parts to lose or break, easy to transport, and impossible to explode. No bulbs or batteries to fail, no mistaking empty fuel tanks either; when a candle's done it disappears. Thus candles lead the pack in foolproof emergency lighting. A 12-inch household paraffin candle will burn for seven or eight hours. Better yet are emergency candles designed for lengthy blackouts. Molded under 1,600 pounds of pressure, these stubby microcrystalline paraffin candles will burn 50 hours or more. Candlelight pales beside lamplight, of course. But it's simple enough to boost illumination by gathering several candlesticks in one place.

A Candle's Worth of Light

Like horsepower, the phrase "candlepower" hangs on in the language if not in science textbooks. Originally it reflected the power of pre-electric light. A candle's worth of light was deemed the fundamental unit of illumination: the sun at its peak produced 600,000 candlepower per square inch, a mantle light up to 100 candlepower, and a kerosene lamp about 5 or 10 candlepower. But the measure suffered from problems of accuracy. A slender beeswax taper is no more kin to a fat tallow candle than a thoroughbred is to a Clydesdale. So a standard candle was established.

Symbol of life, and the most reliable of all firelights, it's even designed to trim itself. As the candle burns, the braided wick twists out of the flame and the residue is incinerated. If some ash does settle on the wax, remove it; otherwise, the candle will gutter and smoke.

Originally it was defined as the luminous intensity of several carbon filament lamps. In 1948 the current standard was adopted: 1/60th of the light intensity emitted by 1 square centimeter of a so-called blackbody (or Planckian) radiator at the temperature at which platinum solidifies (2,046°K). It's called the new international candle, or candela, and has a nicer ring, I think, than *watt*.

Candlepower is good for more than blackouts. Scented with citronella or other insect repellant, a burning candle raises a defense against mosquitoes. A small candle under a kettle heats up a fondue or a stew pot. Sulfur candles are used to fumigate, and perfumed candles burn like incense. In the past, candles have beamed the light to write letters by, and then produced the seal. To light his easel at night, Michelangelo burned a candle in a holder worn on his head. Candles have been exchanged as currency and burned to measure time. Traditionally, eggs as well as wine were graded and inspected by candlelight. In ancient pagan rites and in modern churches, votive candles invoke divine power.

One of the original blessings of candlelight was the simplicity of manufacture. Candles could be molded at home with suet or tallow rendered from a homegrown beast—roughly 300 candles from an ox, for instance. Natural fat candles were valued doubly by early lighthouse keepers. If the food ran out during a storm they could eat the beacons. Today the connection between candlelight and food remains strong. More candles burn in restaurants than at home, and at home most are lit during dinner.

Beeswax

The finest candles of all are made from beeswax. A 12-inch beeswax candle will burn for 10 to 12 hours, several hours longer than a household paraffin candle of equal size. Beeswax candles, which are widely available, have less tendency to drip than paraffin, won't smoke, hold their shape better in hot weather, and yield a steadier flame. Best of all is the fragrance of beeswax, whether it's burning or not: a honey vanilla scent to match its golden color. Candles made from the capping wax that bees use to seal honeycombs burn the brightest and with the richest bouquet. I think the slightly higher cost of beeswax is more than justified by its longer, smokeless burn. And nothing beats beeswax candles for after-dinner marshmallow toasts.

Candle Cautions

There are several elemental precautions for the candle burner. It's important to steer away from excessive heat for candle placement and storage. In a sunny window, for instance, candles may bend. If not straightened, they'll be out of plumb and a nuisance, if not impossible, to burn. Immersion in a pan of warm water will make them pliable enough for straightening. Broken candles can be fixed by melting and resealing cracks after heating in water, or brief exposure to a flame. Wax that is hot enough to liquefy is hot enough to burn the skin, so caution is advised.

CANDLEMAKING

For those interested in making candles at home, craft and hobby shops often stock candle molds, paraffin, beeswax, stearic acid (used in paraffin candles to raise the melting point and subdue smoking), colors, and scents. My friend Gordon Pine likes beeswax candles, but since he burns a dozen a week it gets expensive. So he and his wife economize with a beeswax scented paraffin candle. Here's his recipe:

1½   lbs. paraffin
3   small chunks of beeswax (about half-thumb size; this is a minimum. One can certainly add more. I add beeswax because even a little gives it a better consistency, a better look, and a better feel.)
3   tablespoons stearic acid
Liquid scent and color (cake type) as desired
Prewaxed wick

Melt paraffin and beeswax in a double boiler, add stearic acid, and color/scent as desired. We use three to six two-stick tin molds for 10-inch candles. Pour in mold, let cool, and remove. Makes about 36 candles.

Classic all-purpose holder, this candle pan is sometimes called a "saveall." It's handy for burning stubs that can be collected in the pan. The reflective brass carrying handle is perforated so it can double as a wall bracket.

For outdoor burning, or anywhere in a breeze, a glass hurricane chimney is necessary to protect the flame. A blowing flame gutters, drips, and burns unevenly.

Just about any candle may drip now and then. To catch running wax use a drip dish, or *bobeche*. You can make one by inserting a disk of aluminum foil in the candle holder so a collar of about ½ inch extends beyond the base. Glass bobeches are available too. Candles should not be allowed to burn down to the stub in glass or ceramic candlesticks, as the candlestick is liable to break.

Around the wick at the top of a burning candle is a small pool of hot liquid wax. When you blow out the candle, be careful not to spatter hot wax around. Better yet, extinguish the flame by capping it momentarily with a snuffer. If your local merchant doesn't stock any, try a spoon.

Finally, if you don't like the lingering smoke of a freshly extinguished wick, wet your fingers and give the wick a quick pinch. I enjoy a brief whiff of beeswax candle smoke, but not that of paraffin.

Kerosene and Parrafin Wick Lamps

Not long after moving to the hills I was invited to a neighbor's for a night of music. I'd never been to Martha's and I looked forward to some music and dancing and to seeing her place. It was an old farmhouse, weathered and gray. Dusk was settling when I arrived. I'll never forget the vision as Martha swung open the door. Behind her, covering a round oak table, flamed a constellation of kerosene lamps. They were glass chimney lamps, each one polished diamond bright and filled to the brim with fuel. The room was lit by an orange rainbow. Pumpkin-red flames blossomed over glowing lamp reservoirs, and everyone's face seemed bathed by a Halloween bonfire. Martha had just polished and filled the lamps, and I helped disperse them throughout the house. It was a weekly ritual, she explained, one of the ceremonies of living without electricity.

A while later I cut the electric cord myself. Some of my friends contemplating a backwoods move balked at living non-electrically. I didn't hesitate. That night at Martha's convinced me.

It's been decades since then, the early years illumined solely by kerosene light. Even after I replaced most of the lamps with brighter liquid propane (LP) gas mantle lights I saved several wick burners, and not for nostalgia's sake. Unlike LPs, wick lamps are portable, their light level can be adjusted, and I don't have to worry about broken mantles. I've used kerosene lamps to thaw out frozen water pipes and keep the root cellar from freezing on 30-below nights. And if the LP runs out, kerosene lamps are a must. Best of all, they're inexpensive; many hardware stores carry simple kerosene lamps for about $10 (of course, fancier models and antiques can cost a lot more).

The kerosene wick lamp is the granddaddy of firelight. It hasn't changed significantly since the aerodynamically tapered glass chimney and vented burner were devised more than 150 years ago; before that, the best lamps were little changed from the fat-burning stone cressets of 20,000 B.C. What makes the wick lamp—from the Greek *lampein*—such a masterpiece of timeless design? Simplicity. The ubiquitous, inexpensive wick lamps at the local hardware store and the imposing European antiques all have four basic elements in common: fuel reservoir, burner, cloth wick, and glass chimney.

A wick lamp works quite simply. Fuel in the reservoir, or font as it's sometimes called, is soaked up by a wick that is ignited at the burner. The resulting flame is both protected by the chimney and brightened by it, as the chimney creates a draft. There are some minor subtleties to the process, which we'll get into as we go over a lamp, part by part, and discuss what fuels it. The flames from lamp combustion deliver light equivalent to that of a 25- to 40-watt bulb, and their illumination can be amplified by using a reflector, or a double-wick burner. The light may not be sufficient for detail work, although in a pinch, it's enough for reading. The more lamps, of course, the brighter the illumination.

Fuel

Kerosene is the standard fuel for wick lamps. The term kerosene is used loosely to describe a thin flammable oil with a rather high ignition or flash point, roughly 160°F. That high ignition temperature makes kerosene safer for household use than more volatile alcohol or gasoline—in fact, a lighted match can be dunked in a pot of kerosene without igniting it.

Kerosene and parrafin fuel lamps are distinguished by their wicks and fuel reservoirs. Pictured here left to right are a single wick with transparent glass reservoir, a duplex wick with ceramic reservoir, and a round wick with brass reservoir.

Kerosene can be produced from coal oil, oil shale, and wood fiber, but it is refined from petroleum most commonly. It can also be made in different grades, so not all kerosene is created equal.

Kerosene can be purchased at a gas station out of the pump, by the bottle in a hardware store, or from a catalog or Web site. If you're buying it from the pump, it's likely you'll be purchasing the newest low-sulphur grade (ULSK), which is cleaner than previous classifications like 1-K or K-1. There are also special proprietary blends of kerosene and other lamp and heater fuels available. Make sure you choose one formulated for wick lamp use, and follow the manufacturer's directions.

When I wrote the original version of this book, the kerosene that was available to lamp users was pretty poor, which is to say, high in sulphur and tar. It was smoky, smelly, clogged up wicks, and congealed in the lamp fuel pots. Chimneys had to be cleaned frequently and wicks replaced because they often clogged up before they had much chance to burn. Few of us knew why they were such a nuisance, but I gather one reason was that high sulphur kerosene was also good jet fuel because it lubricated the engines. Take out sulphur and you'd have planes falling out of the skies.

Paraffin

About the same time that cleaner-burning grades of kerosene were being marketed for lamp users, a quite different type of fuel became available: paraffin-based fuel. Paraffin lamp oil is refined from petroleum, and in some of its purest formulations is odorless and smokeless. It's generally more expensive than lighting-grade kerosene, but it makes a very pleasant wick lamp fuel. Paraffin fuel doesn't degrade over time, clog wicks, or smoke even when you blow it out. However, it does have a few quirky characteristics: because it travels more slowly up the lamp wick, it works best when the fuel pot is kept at least half full. It begins to gel at freezing temperatures, and needs to be thawed out for use. (Kerosene doesn't gel until way below zero, which is why it's often used in outdoor heating fuel tanks at trailer parks.) Never use a flame or high heat to thaw out fuel; let it warm up slowly. A lamp burning paraffin puts out a bit more heat than kerosene, which can be helpful during a winter blackout. Because of the higher heat and slow capillary action, however, paraffin fuels are not recommended for Aladdin lamps and some large wick lamps and lanterns. I've been so impressed with the new paraffin oils that I recently bought a couple of new wick lamps to replace my older, kerosene-clogged models, and use them regularly. New lamp fuels are being developed, blended, and marketed, including ethanol-based gels, but it's impossible to keep up with all the various products and terminology. For instance, overseas kerosene is often called paraffin, but here it's an entirely different product. If you want to get really confused, try researching lamp fuels on the Internet. Again, I suggest buying from a reputable local dealer or Lehman's (888-438-5346, www.lehmans.com), and make sure you're getting the proper fuel for your lamp.

Reservoirs

Of course, there's more to lamplighting than burning the right fuel. In choosing the lamp, for example, you can select from several styles of fuel reservoir. The reservoir may be glass, metal, or ceramic. Glass has the most advantages—and liabilities. A glass bowl offers a constant reading on the amount of fuel and the length of the wick. That's helpful, because it's important to maintain at least a half-inch of fuel in order to sustain bright illumination. It's important also to keep a generous length of wick in the bowl for good capillary action. If you're burning several lamps with any regularity, you'll appreciate not having to open up the bowls to check the fuel or the wick. A glass bowl also lets some light through to the tabletop, while a metal or ceramic bowl casts a shadow.

On the other hand, if the glass reservoir breaks you're in trouble: a big mess, or a fire. Still, I prefer glass bowl lamps, perhaps because I've been lucky enough to avoid breakage. Others haven't been as fortunate. According to a report by the Consumer Product Safety Commission on accidental lamp fires, overturned lamps are the major source of injuries.

You can eliminate the risks of glass with an unbreakable metal reservoir. Solid brass, aluminum, or steel coated with enamel, nickel, or brass are used for lamp bowls. One of my first lamps was a 19th century round-wick Vestal with a silver-plated, 1-quart reservoir. It didn't take me long to catch on to the advantage of the ample fuel capacity. A big reservoir reduces the need to refuel, and that's particularly useful when you can't see how much fuel you're burning. I also like the Vestal's separate filling hole, a handy feature on any reservoir. A separate hole makes it easy to use a dipstick for gauging the fuel supply, and simplifies refueling too. Otherwise, reservoirs must be filled by removing the burner and chimney assembly, including the wet wick. However you fill the reservoir, be careful not to overfill it; kerosene expands somewhat as it warms up, and you don't want the lamp to overflow.

I know potters who make exquisite lamp bowls, and indeed many ceramic lamps are available. But I can't see the point of a fragile reservoir that doesn't offer the viewing advantages of glass. If you do happen to chance upon an irresistible ceramic lamp, be sure to check the finish. One Christmas I received a clay lamp that burned brightly that night, but next morning was seeping kerosene onto the table. The potters had neglected the interior glaze.

Burners

Plugged into the top of the fuel pot is a dome-shaped device that brings all the elements of the kerosene lamp into focus: the burner. The burner houses the wick and its height-regulating mechanism, supports the chimney, and holds the flame. Moreover, when the lamp is lighted, the burner draws preheated air through a circular opening just below the flame, thus enhancing combustion. Together with the chimney, the burner transforms an inherently dim, smoky flame into a bright, clear light. And on many lamps, as I said, the burner also serves as the cap to the fuel reservoir.

Burner sizes differ according to the size of the reservoir collar, the chimney base, and the wick width. A Number 1 burner fits a ⅞-inch collar, holds a 2½-inch chimney, and takes a flat ⅝-inch wick. A Number 2 burner fits a 1¼-inch collar, holds a 3-inch chimney and a 1-inch wick. Smaller "Nutmeg" burners fit Number 00 collars and take a ⅜-inch wick and a smaller 1⅛-inch chimney. To protect against corrosion, burners are made of solid brass or brass-plated steel, and are simple to maintain. The kerosene keeps the wick regulating mechanism oiled, and the dome is often hinged for easy access to the wick when it's time for trimming or replacement. With the dome tipped up, you'll see that the circular opening that provides the draft is screened. That keeps wick ashes from falling through the burner. The screen should be cleaned periodically to allow unrestricted air flow. Avoid cheap burners with no protective screening. And make sure not to bend or crimp the wick shaft; the shaft must allow the wick to turn up smoothly to produce an even flame. (One type of lamp, made in Hong Kong and called the Duplex, is fitted with a two-wick burner. The Duplex is highest in candlepower of the flatwick lamps I've used. At this writing, Lehman's is the only source. See "Sources" for more information.)

Wicks

The wick and its turnup wheel are the lamps only moving parts. The wick must fit snugly in the wick mounting, yet be free enough to move and draw a copious flow of kerosene to the flame by capillary action. Over the years, a flat ribbon of woven cotton has proven the easiest to maintain. Tubular wicks are a bit tricky to trim evenly, and it's no cinch to devise a regulating mechanism that lifts the wick symmetrically.

Installing a lamp wick is easier than threading a needle, but not much. It may help to cut a fresh edge on the wick before slipping it into the mounting shaft in the burner. As the wick is fed in, the regulating wheel should be turned until the wick catches and emerges. In particularly tight shafts, it may be necessary to wet the wick in kerosene before fitting.

Duplex (double-wick) burners offer single- or double-wick burning, thus the broadest illumination spectrum in kerosene wick light. Many double wicks have a mechanical snuffer, especially handy on overhead lamps.

The lamp burns best when there is roughly ⅛ inch of fiber topping the shaft—and 3 or 4 inches of wick at the bottom of the fuel pot. The lamp won't burn at its peak candlepower if the wick has only a shallow rooting in the fuel. Besides, you'll have to fill the reservoir constantly just to keep the wick saturated.

Unlike a candle wick, which is woven so that the fiber is consumed in the flame, the lamp wick is not self-trimming. After 20 or 30 hours of normal use, the wick grows charred with the residues of unburned fuel, and the flame dims and smokes. It takes just a moment to extinguish the lamp and cut a fresh edge. To produce an even flame, chop the wick straight across with a pair of scissors (it sometimes helps to cut off the corners first). After trimming, clear any charred remains from the burner screen. I know some people who prefer to clean the wick by simply rubbing off the charred edge with their fingers, or a match, which saves time. To minimize charring, watch that the flame is not set too high. Turned up beyond an efficient level, the lamp's alarm goes off: the flame turns red and begins to smoke.

When you see that it's time to replace the entire wick, remove the burner and use the regulating wheel to eject the old wick.

Chimneys

Topping off the wick lamp is the glass chimney, and like other elements of the lamp it performs several important tasks simultaneously. The chimney creates the draft that increases combustion and brightens the light, and it's also a wraparound windshield to protect the flame.

Straight-sided glass chimneys were first used on wick lamps in the 18th century. Before the close of that century, Aime Argand, a Swiss inventor, with help from a French assistant, discovered that constricting the chimney just above the flame aided combustion and amplified the light. Hence the present-day chimney's graceful taper above the bulbous base. Unlike the hurricane chimney sometimes used to shield candles, the wick lamp's chimney is a necessity. Without it, the lamp would be smoky and dimmer than a candle.

Standard chimneys are made with clear, frosted, or patterned glass and come in several sizes: Number 00, with a 1⅛-inch base or "fitter"" Number 0, with a 1⅝-inch fitter; Number 1, with a 2½-inch fitter; Number 2, with a 3-inch fitter; and Number 3, with a 3½-inch fitter. The largest chimneys, called Store Lamps, have 4-inch fitters.

Chimney heights vary, with 7½ inches to 12 inches being most common. Above an altitude of 4,000 feet, where extra oxygen is needed for combustion, many lamp keepers prefer even taller chimneys.

Chimney glass is tempered for heat resistance, but there's no getting around its fragility. Held in place at the base by an expandable metal ring or several clamps, the chimney is easy to slip off for cleaning, wick trimming, or burner removal; and it stands secure when the lamp is stationary. Nevertheless, the clamp cannot always be counted on when the lamp is being moved. If need be, steady the chimney by holding it at the base, where it may be cool enough to handle.

A lamp that is properly fueled and maintained won't often need chimney cleaning. When it does, a little soap and water is sufficient. To prevent breakage caused by thermal shock when cleaning, be sure to let the chimney cool before dunking it in water. Apart from that, it's possible to dry clean the glass by twisting a wad of newspaper inside the chimney.

When it comes time to blow out the lamp, aim for the chimney top. Cup a hand on the side away from you for best snuffing. To curtail smoking, turn the lamp down low before extinguishing. (The same is true for ignition: let the lamp warm up for a moment before raising the flame.)

Safety Tips and Accessories

Selecting a safe site is perhaps the lamp keeper's greatest responsibility. Sometimes it's not easy to find a spot for the lamp that is both effective for shedding light and out of harm's way. On a kitchen counter, for instance, it may be difficult to light up the sink and also keep the hot chimney protected from splashing water, which could crack the glass. A workbench, where chips are flying, poses a similar threat. Often a lamp bracket solves the problem. Brackets of decorative cast iron can be mounted on wall or post, yielding an extra margin of safety. Lamps designed for hanging are also available. These lamps often include a chimney cap to deflect heat, making them well suited to hang from the ceiling. Remember to follow the lamp maker's specifications for safe clearances to the nearest combustible surface.

Anyone on the lookout for shipboard kerosene lighting will be pleased to hear that gimbal-mounted wick lamps are still made. These lamps remain vertical even when the hull doesn't.

The ability to adjust illumination is one of the highlights of the wick lamp, and the lamp keeper can further extend the light range by using reflectors and shades. Tin-plated steel reflectors or mirrors amplify illumination without burning a drop of extra kerosene. Those who prefer their flames tinted can slip colorful glass shades over the chimney to be supported by a brace on the burner.

Aladdin Light

Bright as a 60-watt bulb, with adjustable illumination, as well as portable, and available in more than a dozen models with better than a dozen shades, and adaptable to electricity: this is the Aladdin, the most versatile kerosene lamp in the world. With a few refinements, it's the same lamp that revolutionized oil lighting more than a century ago, and it is still the Aladdin that many lamp keepers turn to for non-electric lighting. There's no firelight available that burns as brightly without the aid of a pump or pressurized tank. And there's no other lamp as sneaky. If you don't keep a close watch on the Aladdin during warm-up, it can erupt like a volcano, spewing smoke through the house, blacking the mantle with carbon, and perhaps touching off a fire. This is one dimension of the lamp that advertisements don't mention. The reason so many people live with this peril is clearly because Aladdins give a high quality of light when everything is working right.

Lighting with Style

"Aladdin light" is a phrase that describes a special quality of illumination as well as the lamp itself. This is light with a character all its own. The turnup wheel can be spun from dim to dazzling, in contrast to most mantle lamps of fixed candlepower. Moreover, no matter what the setting, the incandescent mantle diffuses the light with an effect similar to that of a frosted light bulb. It is soft, with an ultramarine luster, a light I've heard described as "deep."

And although the light is triggered by a cotton wick burning beneath the mantle, the Aladdin has none of the flicker characteristic of wick lamps. The mantle "freezes" the flame. Flow lines of illumination beam out in a 360-degree flood, although the Aladdin does cast a fuel pot shadow.

The Aladdin is a hybrid. It combines two unique elements of firelight design: the tubular wick and the Welsbach mantle. The tubular cotton wick was devised by Aime Argand, working in France in 1784. It was a terrific advance over the flat ribbon wick, although it proved difficult to perfect. Argand's wick consisted of a ring of cotton wrapped around a central draft tube. The snags involved designing a turnup mechanism that would consistently deliver a symmetrical flame, and solving problems of trimming—troubles that can still pester Aladdins today. Nonetheless, when it worked, Argand's wick delivered 10 to 12 times the customary light from a fuel lamp.

One hundred years after the appearance of the Argand lamp, Austrian chemist Carl Auer von Welsbach invented the incandescent lamp mantle. This is a small gauze pouch impregnated with oxides of rare-earth metals. (This is further described in the "Incandescent Mantle" section.) Heated in a flame, the mantle yields a brilliant light because of the incandescence of the oxides. Little more than a brittle ash, the mantle will not incinerate below the melting point of the materials: 1,750°C. In many lamps, the Welsbach mantle is ignited directly by a gas flame (it was discovered over a Bunsen burner and today shows up also on LP gaslights and Coleman-type gas pressure lamps). However, in the Aladdin, the mantle is ignited by the flame of an Argand-like tubular cotton wick. Hence the unique character of the Aladdin: it's a kerosene lamp that burns as bright as pressurized gas—or an electric bulb.

At the turn of the 20th century, the tubular wick and the Welsbach mantle were first combined in a German lamp called the Practicus. Imported to the United States, the Practicus caught the eye of a young Nebraskan, Victor Samuel Johnson, who saw its potential for rural sales. In 1907, Johnson formed a company in

Kansas City, Missouri, to import and sell the Practicus. Soon there was sufficient business to prompt Johnson to move his outfit to Chicago, where he began work on improving the lamp. To eliminate smoking and unreliability, he acquired a patent for a new lamp burner from an inventor named Charles Wirth, and, in 1909, Johnson introduced the first Aladdin lamp. He named it after the mythical lad in the *Arabian Nights* who won a fortune from a genie in an oil lamp. By 1915, after more improvements in the burner, mantle, and flame spreader, the Aladdin was winning gold medals at international expositions, and Johnson was on his way to his own fortune.

Today, Aladdin sells a lamp that has changed more in style than in substance. The key elements of the Aladdin—the tubular wick and the incandescent mantle—differ little from its turn-of-the-century predecessors. However, the lamp bowl has taken multiple shapes, and many of the early glass models, especially the crystal table lamps made during the 1930s, are now valuable collector's items.

The lamp consists of four basic parts: the reservoir, the burner (which incorporates a tubular cotton wick), the mantle, and the chimney. Aladdin lamps are all quite similar from the burner up (with the exception of various shades). The most significant options involve the reservoir.

The Reservoir

The Aladdin reservoir is produced in a variety of shapes and materials. Reservoirs are made of aluminum, brass, clear glass, and porcelain. There are low reservoirs for the desk or table model reservoirs on 5-inch pedestals, and bowls that can be shifted from table to wall bracket to suspension hanger.

Many people prefer a metal reservoir because it's unbreakable. It's particularly wise to choose metal over glass in the case of Aladdins, because they tend to be more top-heavy than traditional kerosene wick lamps; the pedestal models crowned with a glass shade are especially so. A metal reservoir is cheap insurance against accidental breakage and a flammable fuel spill. Reservoirs of brass or less expensive aluminum are available in the traditional Aladdin styles: the pedestal table model and the desktop. The low boy desk lamp is designed to adapt to a wall bracket or suspension hanger as well, making it the most flexible model.

Aladdin reservoirs are also available in clear and tinted transparent glass and opaque porcelain. The advantage of glass is that the lamp keeper can check the fuel supply at a glance. Because it's especially important to keep the Aladdin from running dry to prevent damage to the wick, a lamp reservoir that doubles as a fuel gauge is a significant convenience. The tradeoff, of course, is that the glass is fragile.

Porcelain reservoirs are attractive, although they seem the worst of both worlds: a fragile bowl that hides the fuel. Even more vexing, most porcelain bowls lack a filling cap. That means the lamp keeper must unscrew the burner from the bowl to fill up, which exposes the wet wick, and special care must be taken to avoid spills. (A filler cap might not be as important on a wick lamp that needs a refueling every 48 hours or so, but the Aladdin burns kerosene four times as fast.)

Because the lamp reservoir accounts for so much of the Aladdin's function, it's easy to customize a lamp by simply screwing on a different reservoir. For instance, you might find a secondhand Aladdin with a pedestal bowl you don't like, or one that lacks a filler cap. For a modest sum you can order a bowl better suited to your lighting requirements.

The Burner

Like the carburetor on a combustion engine or the draft on a wood stove, the Aladdin burner mixes air with fuel to make fire. In the engine, fire is converted to horsepower. In the stove, fire is concentrated for thermal power. In the Aladdin, fire is converted to candlepower. The burner makes it possible for the Aladdin to generate light from a highly efficient mixture of 6 percent kerosene and 94 percent oxygen. Thus, even though you may burn low-

Using the flame of a tubular wick to heat its incandescent mantle, the Aladdin bridges the gap between the classic kerosene wick lamp and the modern mantle light.

grade kerosene, the Aladdin is nearly odorless. (A wick lamp throws off 30 percent of its fuel as unburned vapor; the Aladdin wastes hardly a drop.)

Threaded into the lamp reservoir, the burner sits atop the fuel supply and supports the mantle and chimney gallery. The burner consists of a perforated metal cylinder, a tubular wick and its regulating mechanism, and a flame spreader. Burner design is uniform on all late-model Aladdins, with the options to choose between solid brass and a brass alloy coated with chromium.

The wick draws up fuel by capillary action. At the top of the burner, the wick is exposed about ⅛ of an inch. At the top of the burner, the wick burns with the help of a double draft feeding up through the perforated burner wall. Air rushes to the tubular wick from inside through the flame spreader and from outside through a perforated ring that encircles the wick. As the wick flame warms up, the mantle begins to glow. The hotter the fire, the brighter the light. Unlike a traditional wick lamp, the Aladdin wick burns to make heat, not light.

Today's Aladdin burner is a sophisticated descendant of its original Practicus counterpart. The Practicus burner consisted of a cylindrical wick with a draft tube through the center of the fuel reservoir. The reservoir fit above a pedestal base. At the base of the pedestal was a ring of small vents to draw up air. Adapted to the Aladdin, this center-draft burner remained in place until the 1930s. But there was a problem. The light took 15 minutes or more to stabilize, because air passing through the full length of the reservoir pedestal warmed up so gradually. Hence the lamp keeper had to monitor the Aladdin carefully after ignition. Otherwise, as the temperature rose, the lamp would overheat and flare up.

In 1934, Aladdin introduced the side-draft burner. This new design eliminated the draft tube through the lamp bowl. Instead, the burner drew air through a perforated cylindrical wall above the fuel reservoir. With less mass to steal heat, the Aladdin reached peak illumination in a couple of minutes. The new lamp became known as the "instant light." The side-draft lamp was safer, and because the new burner drew more air to enrich combustion, it brightened the light. The center-draft Aladdin had generated 85 candlepower; the instant light boosted candlepower to 125. The new burner also gave the Aladdin designers greater flexibility. The center-draft lamp had been limited to pedestal models for table use only. But with the side-draft burner, Aladdin reservoirs could be set flat on a table, and moved from desk to wall bracket to pedestal, without disturbing the draft.

At the center of the burner is the tubular wick. The wick consists of a tightly woven cotton tube dangling a pair of cotton tails of a loose weave. The wick fits into the burner so that the tails are immersed in the kerosene while the top is encased in a tubular metal sheathing. The wick is adjusted by means of a rack and pinion mechanism. The rack clips to the base of the tubular wick, which is raised and lowered by the geared wick button. Since 1922, the wicks have been manufactured with an inner and outer reinforcement to prevent deformation and to hold a symmetrical burning edge. The wick's edge is beveled to facilitate installation and cleaning; the wick itself will burn for about a thousand hours.

The flame spreader is the thimble-like cap that fits into the top of the draft tube. Its concave, perforated top deflects air evenly to the surrounding flame. The flame spreader also acts as a protective top on the draft tube, preventing ashes from falling into the burner. During wick trimming, the flame spreader is removed.

The burner is topped by the gallery, a circular twist-on metal ring. Both the mantle and the chimney fit into the gallery, which enables the lamp keeper to remove them for lighting and wick trimming.

The Mantle

The mantle is approximately 3 inches tall, conical, and resembles a spider's web. It is the heart of the lamp, the source of light. The mantle's rare-earth filaments make it possible for an unpressurized kerosene lamp to produce four to seven times the illumination of a customary kerosene lamp.

The mantle is extremely delicate and must be handled with care. In fact, it should not be handled at all. The mantle is framed in a metal structure so you can install it without touching the brittle filaments.

The mantle is the product of an interesting manufacturing process. It begins as a tubular open-weave rayon knitting. This is saturated in a solution of rare-earth chemicals. After drying, the mantle is burned to remove the rayon, and what remains is a delicate metallic web. Finally, the mantle is coated with lacquer for protection during shipping and installation. After fitting the mantle on the gallery, the lamp keeper burns off this lacquer. Henceforth, whenever the mantle is heated by the Aladdin wick, the filaments glow.

The Aladdin mantle is unique. It is roughly double the size of a Coleman or LP lamp mantle. And instead of hanging down under a pressurized flow of flammable vapor, the Aladdin mantle stands upright over the circular wick. Moreover, as part of the gallery, it is the only lamp mantle I know that must be removed temporarily during ignition. Consequently, the Aladdin mantle is subject to more stress than any other. That's why the Aladdin mantle is reinforced by a metal brace, which is also why the mantle is more expensive than others, and why, unless the lamp keeper is careful, the mantle frequently will break.

The Chimney

The Aladdin chimney is easy to recognize. At 12½ inches, it is taller than most lamp chimneys. With only a slight outward curve to accommodate the mantle, it looks more like a glass smokestack than the traditional bell-shaped tapering lamp chimney. This sleek design represents a pinnacle in firelight aerodynamics: the high-velocity draft chimney makes it possible for the Aladdin to burn 94 percent oxygen and 6 percent kerosene, producing 125 candlepower. No other unpressurized liquid fuel lamp delivers such brilliant light.

The chimney fits tightly into the gallery to insure a consistent draft. When it's time to ignite the lamp, chimney and mantle are removed together as part of the gallery and replaced after lighting. The glass is heat resistant, of course, but it doesn't have much resistance to thermal shock. It's a good idea to situate the lamp so that no water splashes on the hot chimney.

It's also important to give the lamp adequate overhead clearance for proper combustion and to insure against overheating and fire. An open chimney should be sited at least 36 inches below any material, combustible or otherwise. Aladdin makes a smoke bell that can be used over the chimney to deflect heat, and Lehman's (888-438-5346, www.lehmans.com) offers smoke bells. One smoke bell fits the hanging lamp, about 4 inches above the chimney. Another smoke bell is designed for wall-mounted lamps. Nevertheless, despite the protection of the smoke bell, be sure that the chimney top is no closer than 30 inches to an overhead surface.

Another optional chimney fitting is the insect screen. This is a mesh chimney cap to protect the mantle. There's little chance that a bug is going to dive down the chimney of a burning lamp. But when the lamp is out, bugs may wander down and break the brittle mantle.

Aladdin also manufactures chimney extensions for high-altitude lamp keepers. A healthy flame needs a good diet of oxygen, and at high altitudes a taller chimney compensates for the thinner air by increasing the draft. This is especially important in the Aladdin because of the high-oxygen/low-fuel carburetion. Otherwise, the lamp is slow to warm up, never yields full illumination, and the mantle carbonizes. Aladdin's high-altitude "Light Booster" is required for proper burning above 4,000 feet elevation. Above 8,000 feet, use two. The "Light Booster" can also be used at sea level to increase illumination as much as 25%. Lehman's also offers both the Aladdin "Light Booster" and chimney extensions of their own design.

An Aladdin lamp can be at home in many locations—on a suspension hanger, a wall bracket (as shown), and a table. There's also a pivoting wall bracket for use in a boat or camper.

Assembly and Lighting

Setting up a new Aladdin is a matter of assembling the four basic lamp elements: reservoir, burner, chimney, and mantle. To begin, the burner is screwed into the reservoir. (If the lamp includes a tripod shade holder, first it must be attached to the lamp between the burner and bowl.)

The mantle is then installed in the burner gallery. Grasp the mantle by the wire frame; do not touch the mantle fabric. The mantle is locked in place by turning it clockwise. The chimney also is fitted to the gallery with a clockwise twist. Be careful not to overtighten the chimney. The base should fit snugly, but with enough leeway to expand and contract with the heat.

Now the lamp should be filled with a good grade of kerosene— or manufacturer approved lamp fuel. Never use gasoline, alcohol, or other dangerous fuels. Neither is the use of scented lamp oil recommended, because additives in the fuel will foul operation of the lamp. Allow the wick to soak up the kerosene for at least one hour before ignition; the wick must be completely saturated to burn correctly.

Next, burn off the mantle's protective lacquer. Remove the chimney and hold a lit match near the bottom of the mantle, but do not touch the fabric. The protective coating will burn off in a flash. To keep from smoking up the house, and your lungs, do this outside whenever possible, making sure the mantle is protected from the wind. Replace the chimney.

When you want to light the Aladdin, remove the gallery, mantle, and chimney as one unit. Turn up the wick about 1/8 inch above the outer wick tube, and ignite with a match. Allow the flame to cover the entire top edge of the wick, and then carefully replace the gallery assembly and lock it into place. Slowly turn up the wick until part of the mantle glows white. Let the lamp warm up for several minutes. Never turn up the lamp to brightest light immediately because this will cause the lamp to flare up and smoke. After the burner has warmed up fully, the heat generated

The "gallery" holds the mantle (shown here installed) and the chimney, which can be removed for cleaning. The gallery, with mantle and chimney in place, must be removed each time the lamp is lit. Caution: When you are relighting after short intervals, the gallery may be hot.

If a flare-up occurs, do not sprinkle salt down the chimney, as many old-timers recommend. The salt will corrode the burner. Instead, turn the lamp down low and allow the flame to erase the carbon slowly.

will cause the mantle to increase the intensity of its glow. Correct lighting is attained with an illuminated mantle that displays no points of orange flame breaking through the mantle. If flames appear, the wick should be turned down.

To extinguish the lamp, turn the wick down just below the wick tube until the flame disappears. Blow softly into the burner or across the top of the chimney. Then raise the wick to see that the lamp is out. (Some experienced users recommend lowering the wick after use to prevent fuel from puddling on the bottom of the burner.) If you want to light the Aladdin again soon, beware. The gallery will be hot.

The Aladdin requires fresh air, and so does the lamp keeper. Best results will be obtained in well-ventilated areas. Never use a lamp in a sealed area where oxygen is short and carbon monoxide fumes can gather.

It's important to maintain safe distances between the lamp and any combustible surfaces or materials. A clearance of at least 30 to 36 inches above the top of the chimney is recommended by the manufacturer. Always allow adequate space around the lamp to prevent excessive heat buildup.

If you are using a shade, be careful during warm up; the mantle will be invisible. In addition, handling a shaded lamp may be awkward during ignition. Remove the gallery with care.

Maintenance

The Aladdin must not be allowed to burn dry. This would damage or destroy the wick. The flame spreader must be kept clean. If it becomes dented or damaged, replace it. If the mantle becomes blackened from soot or carbon, it should be cleaned by turning the flame down low and letting the crust burn off slowly.

The wick should be cleaned only if it has a formation of carbon crust on the edge. To clean, remove the gallery assembly and turn down the wick until the top edge is even with the wick tube. Remove the flame spreader, and insert the disk-shaped wick cleaner that comes with the lamp into the wick tube. Turn up the wick until it presses gently against the cleaner. Now slowly turn the cleaner clockwise until the wick is smooth. Do not ruffle or gouge the edge, because a ragged wick will produce an uneven flame.

Lantern Light

Firelight is a natural for outdoor illumination, but, as you may have discovered, not just any lamp will do. Take a table lamp outside and it's likely to flicker, smoke, and die in the breeze. These lamps are designed to burn in still air where the chimney draft is steady and undisturbed. And if you've ever tried to navigate a dark trail with a table lamp in hand, you'll know how difficult it is to see beyond the glare of the flame. Moreover, an uncapped chimney is open to precipitation, and foul weather will extinguish the lamp or perhaps crack the hot glass. Glass bowl lamps are fragile besides, and risky for outdoor use.

Outdoors and Portable

Wherever there's a need for outdoor portable light, you're likely to see a fuel-burning lantern—either a high-powered mantle lantern or a simpler kerosene wick burner. Battery-powered flashlights and lamps are fine for short-term use, but nothing beats a lantern for bright, inexpensive, stormproof illumination, whether for camping or general-purpose use around the house or farm. A gas or kerosene pressure lantern will generate more than 200 candlepower—at least the equivalent of a 100-watt light bulb—and burn for eight hours per filling. A kerosene wick lantern will generate up to 12 candlepower and burn for approximately 40 hours each filling.

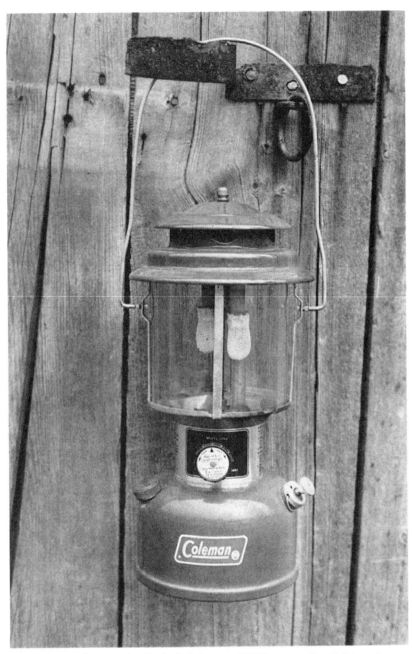

The Coleman lantern is a little lighthouse. Within a weathertight enclosure, its twin mantles generate up to 200 candlepower. And better than a lighthouse, it's portable.

A lantern is a miniature lighthouse. In a kerosene wick lantern, the weatherproof draft system draws oxygen to the wick flame, and the exhaust rises through a perforated, lidded chimney top. A gas or kerosene pressure lantern with mantle features a similar protective chimney, although the brighter mantle light is fed by a vaporous combination of compressed air and fuel. (Pressurized fuel cartridge lanterns are also available.) Both wick and mantle types incorporate glass chimneys specially tempered for resistance to impact and temperature shock. The lantern body is unbreakable steel. A hinged "bail" similar to a bucket handle enables the lamp keeper to carry the lantern below eye level, so that light falls on the terrain without any blinding glare.

The Pressure Lantern

The name Coleman is synonymous with pressure lanterns. Since 1905, the Coleman Company has been producing lanterns in its Wichita headquarters; currently they sell a million or so annually. The company makes several lantern models, including bottled propane lights, but they are known primarily for the quick or instant light pressure lanterns, which feature a hand pump on the fuel tank and burn kerosene or Coleman gas, an unleaded gasoline sold in the familiar red cans found in most camping and general supply stores. Like the Aladdin table lamp, the Coleman pressure lantern is based on a patented design, and it is unique in its field.

The first Coleman lanterns appeared at the turn of the century to compete with several emerging illumination systems. At the time, kerosene, natural gas, and manufactured coal gas fueled a new generation of indoor lamps featuring the Welsbach mantle, and Edison's electric light was catching on. But the mantle lamps were limited to a maximum output equivalent to approximately 75 watts per unit, and early electric light bulbs barely exceeded 25 watts. An empty spot at the high end of the spectrum beckoned: a powerful light for street, store, church, meeting hall, and lighthouse, as well as for farmers and others who worked outdoors.

The Coleman lantern filled that spot. The first Colemans burned a pressurized gasoline vapor produced by hand pumping an air compressor and then preheating a vaporizing generator with an alcohol torch. Once ignited, the gasoline vapor heated an incandescent Welsbach mantle that provided the light: the heat also sustained the vaporizing process.

What caused the Coleman to be so much brighter than other lights? Primarily it was the built-in air pump, which pressurized the pedestal fuel tank to roughly 40 pounds per square inch, creating a fuel-injected light. Combined with the vaporizing effect of the pressurizer and the highly volatile gasoline, the Coleman was quite simply the hottest lamp around—and the higher the heat, the brighter a mantle would shine. Early Colemans delivered approximately 750 candlepower of bright white light from a durable 10-pound unit that could stand on its pedestal tank or hang suspended. In 1905, Coleman lamps illuminated the first night football game, in Wichita. The light was so effective that some people complained it was too bright for household use.

By 1914, Coleman was producing the world's first stormproof pressure lanterns, lit by double mantles. Toward the end of World War I the company introduced its first "Quick Light," incorporating a new generator that could be match lit, quite an improvement over alcohol torch ignition. The lantern grew especially popular with merchants and farmers, and during World War II "Coleman" became part of the language for a whole generation of Americans—the GIs. Coleman devised a pocket stove that became an essential ingredient in many GI packs, and the company received a special government award for its contribution to the war effort.

Indeed, there's something about a Coleman that reminds me of battle. It was at a barn dance on the Fourth of July, years ago, that I lit one for the first time; upon ignition, the lantern flared up like a Roman candle. A plume of fire shot up and singed my eyebrows before I ducked and shut the valve. Then a funny thing happened. The lantern began to glow. Hesitantly, I reopened the valve. Light! That night a single lantern illuminated the cavernous barn, and after midnight we carried it outside, despite the

A Coleman can be a farmer's best friend during a power outage.

rain, to help get our fireworks show off the ground. Later on I learned that an initial flare-up is part of many gas pressure lamp ignition routines. Fortunately, I also learned to minimize the size of the fireball. But I continue to keep my head back and I still handle Colemans like Roman candles.

Safe Handling

There are two types of Coleman pressure lanterns—gasoline and kerosene. Both are fundamentally similar, incorporating hand-pressurized fuel tanks and one or two mantles. But each fuel demands its own distinct ignition procedure. The gasoline lantern offers the easiest start-up, but because of the highly flammable fuel it calls for the most cautious handling. The kerosene lantern is the trickiest to light, but the low flash point of the fuel makes it the safest. Illumination is slightly higher with the gasoline double-mantle lantern; the cost per hour is slightly lower for the single-mantle kerosene lanterns.

It is absolutely crucial to know what you're doing when you operate a Coleman lantern. The combination of pressurized flammable fuel—especially gasoline—and a tricky ignition procedure that often involves a momentary burst of flame may cause injury or property damage if you do not follow instructions. The instruction pamphlets provided with each lantern all begin with boldface warnings, which can be condensed as follows:

- Do not use in unventilated areas.
- Use for lighting only.
- Never fill lantern or loosen or remove fuel cap while lantern is lighted, near flames or other ignition sources, or while top of lantern is hot to touch.
- Never allow any flammable material to come within 2 feet of the top and 1 foot of the side of the lantern.
- Replace any mantle with a hole in it.
- Never adjust light output with fuel valve or cleaning lever.
- Keep out of reach of children.
- In the case of gasoline lanterns, use only Coleman fuel or clean, fresh white gas. Never use fuel containing lubricating oils, lead compounds, or other metallic compounds. (Some unleaded automotive fuels may contain metallic compounds.) Coleman fuel is extremely flammable. Use the same care as when using gasoline.
- For kerosene lanterns, use only clean, fresh white kerosene.

Coleman makes several pressure lanterns: both double- and single-mantle gasoline burners and single-mantle kerosene lanterns. One of their most popular lanterns is the double-mantle gas model. Its 1-quart fuel capacity generates eight hours of 220 candlepower light. The lantern stands 14 inches high and weighs 5 pounds. Except for the mantles, the lantern comes pre-assembled.

Fueling

Whether you burn Coleman gas, white gas, or kerosene, it's a good idea to get in the habit of pouring the fuel through a filtered funnel. That will minimize the buildup of deposits in the generator, which leads to lower efficiency and eventual replacement of the generator. Before filling, close both the fuel valve and the pump knob firmly. During filling, the lantern should be in a level position. Tighten the fuel cap firmly after filling, and wipe up any spilled fuel.

Mantles

Unscrew the ball nut at the top of the lantern so you can remove the ventilator top and the glass globe. Then tie the mantles on with the strings tight around the grooves in the burner caps. Distribute the folds evenly. The flat side of each mantle should face the generator. Cut off surplus string. Always use Coleman mantles, which are designed for use with high-pressure fuel; LP tie-on mantles are larger, with a looser weave, and will not work properly. Now burn off the protective mantle coating by lighting—without touching the bottoms of the mantles. This should be done in a well-ventilated area, or outside, to clear the smoke. Be sure that the mantles are burned until only a white ash remains. Allow the mantles to cool before lighting the lantern. The mantles are very fragile and must not be touched. Now reassemble the lantern.

Pumping

With the fuel valve firmly closed, open the pump knob one turn. Closing off the hole in the knob with your thumb, pump approximately 35 strokes. (If the lantern is not full of fuel, more strokes are required.) Now close the knob firmly. Good air pressure is essential to lantern operation. In older lanterns, the leather in the pump seal may dry out and require oiling to hold air. To test the seal, close the pump knob firmly, place your thumb over the hole, and pump. If you feel little or no resistance, remove the pump, work several drops of oil into the leather, and replace the pump.

Lighting the Gas Coleman

Move the cleaning lever to the down (open) position. Insert a lighted match through the lighting hole at the base of the globe. Hold it near (without touching) the mantle, and now open the fuel valve ¼ turn only. The mantle will take a few seconds to light, during which there will be a burst of flame. When the mantle glows brightly—but with no flames—open the fuel valve fully. For good air pressure, pump up an additional 15 to 25 strokes, following the pumping method previously outlined. After the lantern has started, and whenever necessary during operation, rotate the cleaning lever several times to clean deposits from the generator, then leave it in the down position. Keep in mind that additional pumping will be necessary at intervals during operation.

Extinguishing

Rapidly rotate the cleaning lever several times and leave in the down position. Close the fuel valve firmly. The lantern will dim and go out in a half-minute or so.

Kerosene Lanterns

Kerosene-burning Colemans operate essentially the same as gas burners, with the exception of lighting. In the case of one model, a preheater cup is filled with alcohol (not gasoline or kerosene), which is match lit through the lighting hole. The flame then is allowed to consume nearly all the alcohol before the fuel valve is opened and the lantern lights. In the case of another, a squeeze bulb is provided with the lantern. Two bulbfulls of kerosene are squirted onto the wick material inside a preheater cup and screen. The kerosene must soak into the wick for one minute or so. The kerosene then is lit through the lighting hole, and the flame allowed to burn for 90 seconds. Then the fuel valve is opened and shut immediately. If the mantle burns brightly with no smoke, the valve can be opened fully. If smoke and soot billow up, extra pre-heating will be needed before opening the fuel valve.

Trouble Shooting

Flames other than at the mantle indicate flooding or a leak. Close the fuel valve firmly. Permit the flames to burn out and allow the lantern to cool. In the case of flooding, wipe up the fuel and start again. Otherwise, check for leaks and repair. If the lantern dims, pump in more air and give the cleaning lever a few spins. Leave the lever in the down position. If the lantern sputters or loses efficiency, or the mantles turn black, the generator may be clogged and need replacement. (Be sure to rinse the lantern fuel tank occasionally with fresh fuel to remove sediment, gum formations, and moisture accumulations; clean out the burners once a year.)

Oil the pump leather periodically to maintain the seal.

Indoor Gas Pressure Lamps

Coleman lanterns are intended primarily for camping and outdoor use, and indoor use is not recommended. However, at least one independent manufacturer has designed a pressurized fuel lamp for indoor use. Bright it may be, but the risk of using highly flammable fuel indoors seems hardly worth it.

The Kerosene Wick Lantern

It's not always necessary, or even desirable, to stoke up a Coleman for outdoor light. In some situations the Coleman is downright overpowering. You can't turn down a gas pressure Coleman—it's either on or off. Who wants a hissing, blinding beacon on the picnic table in the evening, when a quiet, flickering wick lantern will do? Or when a long-running, low-key, fuel-efficient light is all that's required? Besides that, mantle lanterns are poorly suited to rough handling. It's true that the lantern housing is sturdy and stormproof, but it doesn't take much of a jolt to break the mantle, and that means replacement because even a small hole in the mantle will tend to overheat and crack the globe.

The Dietz lantern

Hence, the kerosene wick lantern, known to many people as the trainman's lantern or hurricane lamp, is preferred. It's hard to top for all-around outdoor light. It's not as bright as a Coleman, but it's simple to operate, safe, and inexpensive—three qualities that go a long way in the country. Essentially, the wick lantern is an oil lamp inside a stormproof housing. But instead of removing the chimney to light it, the glass is lifted with a built-in lever. Otherwise, it is operated in the same manner as a kerosene wick lamp.

The Dietz Company, originally of New York has more than a century's experience in the kerosene lantern business. Today, the Dietz lanterns are most likely the sturdiest available. The Dietz Air Pilot generates 12 candlepower for 45 hours per filling. And if you're looking for light with an extra flair, in addition to clear globe glass, they offer red.

Liquid Propane Gaslight

What is it about gaslight that puts it at the top of the list of non-electric lights? For one thing, a well-maintained gaslight delivers at least the equivalent of a 50-watt incandescent bulb, and that's minimum. I find it's usually closer to 75 or 100 incandescent watts. (With the advent of fluorescent lights, the watt as an illumination standard is somewhat outmoded; nevertheless fluorescent bulb manufacturers continue to use watts as an equivalency index, and so will I.) Just as important as brightness is the constancy of light. Kerosene or white gas mantle lamps can generate as much light as a gaslight, but not on a continual basis, without periodic tinkering, refilling, and/or pumping. It's the steady feed of pressurized LP gas that makes for steady light. And there's no chance of a flare-up due to overheating.

In addition to its uniform quiet light, the gaslight is bright by design. With LP gas piped to the light, there is no fuel reservoir forming the base as is customary on most firelights. That eliminates the characteristic shadow that falls below most fuel pot lamps. Anyone familiar with Colemans, Aladdins, and wick lamps will appreciate this design superiority.

In addition, because of the steady fuel pressure and the permanent mounting, the delicate mantle is unlikely to break.

An Economical Solution

Right now in my neighborhood in central Vermont, LP ranges between $2.25 and $2.77 a gallon, depending on the dealer and the amount of gas consumed. (Ironically, those who conserve pay the most, and those who burn the most pay the least.)

A gaslight will run approximately 48 hours on a gallon of LP gas—that's 12 hours per pound. To figure out your hourly running cost, divide the price per gallon by 48. My dealer charges $2.45 a gallon delivered. That means I'm paying just over $0.05 per hour. When I used gas lights for primary lighting, I estimate I burned an average 15 hours of light a night (three lights, for instance, each burning five hours), which would now cost me about $0.75 a night, $22 a month, or about $264 a year.

It's interesting to compare running costs for electric and gaslight. The electric rate here is $0.12 per kilowatt hour plus a daily $0.38 surcharge. Say a 100-watt bulb will run for $.012 an hour. At first it appears that gaslight costs almost five times as much as electric. But if you take into account the electric company's surcharge, about $11 per month, think of how much extra gaslight you could buy every month without that extra fee: about 4 gallons of propane, worth 192 hours of light. That's close to two weeks of gaslight at the daily 15-hour average. Using fluorescents will of course cut electrical costs; but if you're living without electricity, or the power goes out, fluorescent electric lights won't banish the dark, no matter how efficient they are.

How about LP compared to kerosene, Coleman fuel, or white gas? I found that none of those fuels burns significantly brighter than LP, yet the fuel is often two or three times as expensive. Other factors in cost comparisons include the gaslight itself, tubing, and installation. Again, gaslight compares favorably with its closest indoor competition, the Aladdin. A single gaslight will cost between $75 and $100 or so, plus the price of a few yards of copper tubing and installation costs, if you ask your gas dealer to do the work.

To ignite liquid propane, strike a match, hold it close under the mantle without touching it, and turn on the gas.

Here's another way to look at the economics of gaslight: bar-gain-hunting land buyers are savvy about the price savings in real estate that's not served by electricity.

Safety

Fire and fumes are two hazards usually associated with com-bustible lighting. For the most part these hazards are eliminated by gaslight design. According to the U.S. Consumer Protection Agency, most lamp fires occur when a burning light is upset. This is a real danger with table lamps, but not with LP gaslights, which are permanently mounted on the wall or ceiling.

Another frequent cause of fire is lamp flare-up. This happens when a fuel lamp overheats, usually during warm up or in a poor-ly ventilated space. This cannot happen with an LP gaslight because the rate of combustion is governed by tank pressure and the lamp valve.

Fires can also start when a lamp is set near a flammable mate-rial. But when installed properly, following the manufacturer's clearance recommendations, a gas lamp burns within its own safe-ty zone, like a wood stove.

I've been asked if there isn't a chance that a burning gaslight might go out and fill the house with a cloud of explosive and toxic gas. Sure it's possible. But nothing close to that happened to me during more than a decade of gaslighting, perhaps because we had an inviolable house rule: never leave a burning light unattended.

I have heard of explosions in homes using gas that is piped in from a different source. These result from disruptions in the sup-ply line. Such an accident is highly unlikely with LP gas, because the household fuel supply is on-site, and under your control. It's even possible to shut off the outdoor gas tank when you're not using the lights or other appliances. This is a nuisance, and we didn't do it.

When fuels burn incompletely, as almost all fuels do to some extent, toxic carbon monoxide gas is produced. You can't see, taste, or smell carbon monoxide, but it can make you sick or kill you. A gaslight is designed to burn at a fixed rate, with no adjustments in the level of illumination. Thus, by design, it is tuned to burn at peak combustion efficiency, minimizing the production of carbon monoxide. Unfortunately most gaslight manufacturers are reluctant to be specific beyond recommending adequate ventilation. A lighting company engineer once told me: "We'd lose our credibility if we started setting ventilation standards." You can take "adequate" ventilation to mean two things: enough air for the light to burn properly, and an air exchange rate generous enough to exhaust fumes.

Before the advent of tight houses, natural air leakage in a home usually provided enough ventilation. Today, the question of ventilation is more important. After talking with several gaslight manufacturers and an importer of lighting accessories, I'd say that the consensus on gaslight ventilation rates hovers between 2 and 3 cubic feet of air per hour per light. In old (leaky) homes, natural air exchange should be more than enough for several gaslights. To ventilate airtight houses, a nearby window should be left open slightly at top and bottom. A carbon monoxide detector should be installed in areas where gaslights are used, with new batteries regularly put in.

"We're trying to steer away from RVs, camper caps, and ice shanties," one manufacturer explained to me.

Location and Installation

The typical gaslight has four main working parts: the valve and wall bracket assembly, the valve cover, a glass globe, and a mantle. You can put a gaslight together in a couple of minutes, and, with the unit unconnected, move it around to judge how it will fit in various locations. If you haven't seen a gaslight working, check one out; it will make it easier for you to locate your light in a good spot. Remember: gaslights and tubing are permanently mounted, and changing locations can be troublesome and expensive.

There are several manufacturers of gaslights for indoor use. The Humphrey is a popular gaslight in the United States. This is the

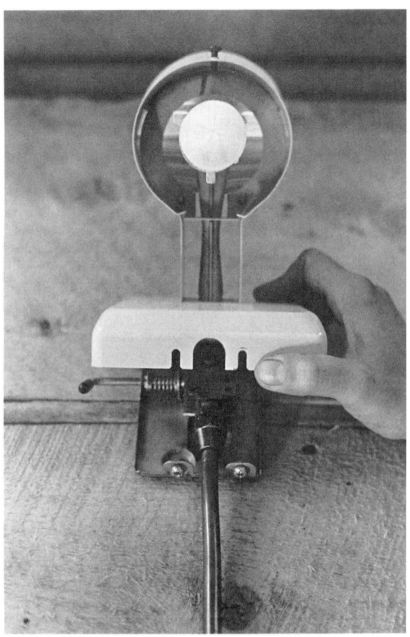

Liquid propane gaslight anatomy. The wall bracket is the base of the unit and contains the threaded flare fitting for the upper supply line, the nozzle, and the on/off switch. The valve cover fits over the wall bracket and contains the Bunsen, the burner nose, the mantle, the globe support, and an integral reflector that doubles as a heat shield.

model we once used and it is still available, so it's the one I'll refer to. (See "Sources" for several other gaslight manufacturers.)

Safety, illumination, and economy are the three main considerations when locating a lamp. The mantle is fragile—whether or not it's burning—and the glass globe is fragile too. So your lamp should be outside busy household traffic patterns, and away from work areas where percussion or vibration may cause damage (a workbench, for example). Liquid splashing on a hot gaslight can crack the globe, and a strong current of air can cause the light to pulsate, so keep locations a safe distance from kitchen sinks and cross-drafts.

Most important, follow or exceed the manufacturer's clearance specifications. One gaslight can generate 1,800 Btu every hour, and the temperature just above a light will be about 240°F. Humphrey recommends a clearance of 4 inches between a lamp and any combustible material, but I sited the light in my studio 7 inches below a maple bookshelf, and I wouldn't get any closer.

At first glance a gaslight looks much like a traditional kerosene mantle lamp, but a closer look reveals a twist: the mantle is inverted. Upon ignition the direction of illumination is downward. Keep this in mind as you consider sites.

Note also that the Humphrey globe is divided into a northern hemisphere of frosted glass and clear glass below, as are the globes for most other brands. Thus, it is possible to locate lights at varying heights, depending on the objective (table or desk work, reading, general illumination), and prevent glare. The globes on most LP gaslight brands are interchangeable.

To make room for the gas line there's a punch-out opening at the bottom of the valve cover. You'll want to be sure that a wall light mounts on a flat surface with no obstructions to the tubing or pipe. There is a fitting available that makes it possible to run the gas line inside a wall, but I never liked the idea. It makes alterations in light placement difficult, but even worse, who wants to tear out the wall to check for a leak? Moreover, building codes in some areas prohibit interior wall piping to prevent accidental puncture by nails, screws, etc. Copper tubing is also prohibited in some areas because of its vulnerability to damage.

Humphrey also makes a hanging assembly for ceiling suspended lighting, so that one, two, or three lights can be hung from an overhead position. This is especially helpful in kitchens, where a light over a work surface or table may be handy. The ceiling assembly includes a cover for an interior wall gas hookup, but again I'd recommend against it.

Another way to get around the limitations of a wall mount is to use a pole or post. Two out of three gaslights in my house were mounted on structural posts, and I sited them so that the backlight ordinarily lost on a wall doubles their illuminating effect. One was mounted on a post in the central room, with the forward light flow on the living area and the backlight on the dining table. The other was mounted on a post between the kitchen counter and the living room area.

In an L-shaped room, mounting a light on one side of the inside corner adds roughly 45 degrees of illumination. Even better, it's possible to devise a mounting base for the corner so that a maximum of backlight falls equally to the left and right.

Once your light sites are chosen, you can have an LP dealer install the lamps and tubing, and if necessary, an LP tank. If you have an LP gas tank setup already, your dealer can splice the light tube into the existing piping. A cutoff valve to the lights will enable you to repair or change lamps without shutting off all gas appliances. Be sure to ask if your dealer has experience installing gaslights. It's worth asking around to make sure you don't hire a novice.

If you don't have a gas tank already, the most popular location for one is usually on the backside of the house, for appearance sake. Just make sure there will be year-round access for the supply truck. In northern climates, avoid sites where the tank will be buried in snow. In very cold weather (below -32°F) LP ceases to vaporize, and the light dims. LP tanks should always be outside for safety reasons.

Mantles: Tie-On and Preformed

After your lamps are installed, they are ready for mantles. There are two types of mantles: tie-on and preformed. Each requires a different burner nose on the lamp. The tie-on is less expensive, but it's a little tricky to attach. The preformed mantle is easy to attach, but it's more delicate and expensive. I prefer the tie-on, although it may take you a few tries to get the hang of it. Because the tie-on is unbreakable before burn-off, and slightly flexible after, it's recommended for RVs.

No matter which type of mantle you use, it's necessary to burn off the lacquer coating that protects the delicate fabric before use. The burn-off lasts several minutes, producing a smoky and perhaps unhealthy cloud that I didn't want in the house. What I did was fire up the mantle outside while it was attached to the valve cover assembly. Manufacturers recommend lighting the mantle upside down, holding the match near the top so a slow burn-off burns downward, preventing a flare-up. To be safe, place the assembly on an inflammable surface during burn-off, step back, and wait until the flame and smoke die out after the lacquer coating has burned. Now replace the valve cover assembly very gently on the wall bracket and tighten the screws. (If you don't handle the mantle gingerly, it will break.) If you choose instead to preburn the mantle inside, do it with the windows open.

What you have after the burn-off is a fragile, incandescent chemical ash that will glow in the heat of the burning gas vapor. (Initially, the tie-on will appear a bit misshapen after burn-off, but the first time the light is ignited it will shrink to its final form.)

Lighting

Turning the light on is easy. First, turn on the gas supply at the tank. Next, with the handle of the lamp in the off position, hold a lighted match just under the mantle, and turn the gas on. You will have to depress the handle to release the safety lock. The first time

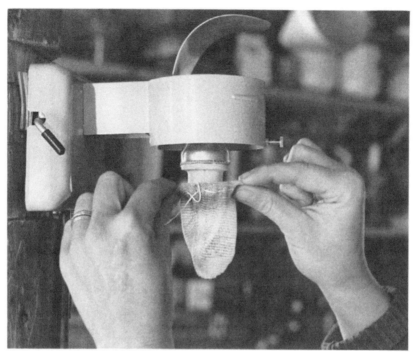

To install a tie-on mantle, tie the strings at the throat of the mantle over the ceramic burner nose and seat in the lower groove. The mantle must be distributed evenly around the burner nose. Pull the ends of the string so that the mantle and string are seated securely in the groove. Tie a double knot and clip off the excess string. After burn-off, it will shrink to its final form. Unlike the preformed mantle, the tie-on is manufactured in a flexible condition and is good for moving vehicles.

you use the light, there may still be some air in the line, so you may need to light several matches. To extinguish the light, return the handle to the off position.

Be careful not to overload your gas appliances. A single tank may not deliver sufficient pressure to power a house full of gaslights, gas stoves, gas water heaters, and so forth. If you see your lights fade when other gas appliances are burning, you may wish to supply the lights from a tank of their own.

The preformed mantle is simple to install: Lift the mantle by its porcelain base ring onto the burner nose and turn until it is seated. Do not touch the mantle! A preformed mantle requires a corresponding burner nose. Before use, the preformed mantle is more fragle than a tie-on.

Gaslight maintenance is no big chore: clean the glass globe occasionally and replace the mantle when it breaks. Check the burner nose periodically to make sure it's tight; the gasket tends to shrink with use.

I can still remember the first time I lit up a gas lamp. There was a muffled pop like a champagne cork, and a wave of light bathed the room. It was remarkably bright, with a warmth unmatched by electric lights. For a minute a low growl accompanied the glow as the lamp warmed up. Then the sound ebbed to the faint breeze of gas feeding the flame. It reminded me of the sound of a seashell at my ear.

Incandescent Mantles

Imagine the delight of a 19th-century lamp keeper upon discovering the newly invented Welsbach mantle. At that time fuel lamps burned at 30 candlepower, tops. Then along came a little thimble-shaped device suspended in the lamp flame that doubled or tripled illumination, and cut fuel consumption to boot—often at a rate between 300 and 400 percent. Who could resist? And indeed, after its patenting in 1885, the incandescent mantle beamed its way into millions of lives all over the planet, rescuing fuel lighting from the dark ages, saving eyesight, and conserving costs.

Radioactive Thorium

Nowadays, millions of mantle lamps are in use annually in the United States alone, and a large percentage of the world's population lights by fire.

Suspended at the center of our brightest non-electric lights—Aladdin, LP, and gas pressure lanterns—is the mantle. And until recently, most mantles were composed of 99 percent thorium and 1 percent cerium, which meant the mantle emitted radiation. It was a fact you weren't likely to read about in lamp ads, but it was also no secret. Any decent encyclopedia will tell you that thorium is a naturally radioactive rare-earth metal, soft, lustrous, and silver white. It can be found abundantly in Brazil, India, Canada, and in especially large deposits in New Hampshire. It is the most stable of the 12 known radioactive isotopes. During its decay, thorium emits both alpha and beta radioactive particles.

What does this mean to the mantle user? Is there a health risk associated with mantle use? I asked this question in 1984, in the first edition of this book, and did my best to come up with the answers. Clearly, there were enough concerns about mantle radioactivity to prompt many lamp manufacturers to eventually substitute a non-radioactive rare-earth metal for the ubiquitous thorium. By the late 1990s, the non-radioactive metal yttrium was beginning to replace thorium in many lamp mantles. Today, companies like Coleman, Aladdin, and Humphrey have removed thorium mantles from their lamps. However, there are some mantle lamp users who prefer the quality of illumination in the thorium mantle, and because some thorium mantles are still available, and quite legal, they continue to be sold.

Because the thorium mantle is still available from some suppliers, and because some people prefer its quality of light, and finally because as many people argue, you're exposed to more naturally occurring radiation at Denver's high altitude than from a dozen mantle lamps, I think the following look at the pros and cons of the thorium mantle is still important.

Before delving into the invisible realm of radioactive isotopes and millirems, it may be useful to have some background on the delicate network of metallic ash filaments we call the mantle. The mantle is the handiwork of chemist Carl Auer von Welsbach, born in Austria in 1858.

Scientific American introduced its readers to his invention in 1887, reporting on a mantle demonstration at the Marlborough Gallery in London. Welsbach mantles attached to the gallery's ordinary gas fittings "emitted a white and brilliant light resembling somewhat of an incandescent electric lamp." It was the mantle's power to challenge electric light that excited people. Six years before von Welsbach's invention, Thomas Edison had introduced his incandescent electric light. Initially it appeared that Edison's new light would easily overshadow the country's fuel lamps. However, the mantle turned out to be even brighter than electric light. Eventually, of course, electric light grew brighter and moved into the majority of homes—at least in the industrialized world. Nevertheless, today the mantle lamp lives on in rural homes, vacation camps, boats, and recreational vehicles.

Dangerous Fallout?

I first became aware of a question of mantle safety not long after buying my first LP lamps. A rumor began to circulate among my neighbors that the smoke from mantle burn-off was dangerous, but it never amounted to more than a rumor. Certainly nothing on the mantle package hinted at trouble. In fact, the only caution associated with firelight came in the LP gas lamp installation instructions that warned against carbon monoxide fumes. But this, I knew, was a potential problem for all fuel lamps, with or without mantles, and proper ventilation was the straightforward solution. Nevertheless, as I had recently installed my first LP mantle lamps, I started to investigate.

Initially, I talked to Herb Rosenhagen, president of Humphrey Products at the time, the manufacturer of my gaslights. I asked him about the rumors I'd heard that mantles might be toxic. He said that several years earlier he had read a newspaper story warning of the dangers of mantle burn-off.

"There may have been a problem," he explained, "but not with our mantles." He sent a follow-up letter detailing the mantle scare. It seemed that a student in California who had written his master's thesis on mantles had stated that the burn-off was harmful. His report was picked up by a newspaper and created some alarm. Rosenhagen decided to get a full analysis of the Humphrey mantles, which were then manufactured by the Falk Company in England. Analysis was performed by Wilmar Associates of Houston, Texas, and issued in a report dated December 12, 1973.

The gist of the study is that a highly toxic metal, beryllium, is the constituent in question:

When incinerated there is no question that beryllium could be toxic. However, tests have been run on old mantles that did contain some beryllium in the hardening solution, and it was found that its content in the burned mantles was less than 50 ppm (parts per million). Under no circumstances could the same concentration be toxic.

Falks mantles do not have beryllium. Basically a mantle is made with thorium and cerium hydroxide impregnated in a viscose rayon fabric, but on soft mantles a hardening solution containing aluminum and magnesium is applied to the top of the mantle and the area of this application is indicated by the dyed section of the mantle. A spectrograph analysis of the ash on a burned mantle shows about 99.26 percent thorium oxide. The balance of material in the mantle is listed as follows: cerium, 1,000 ppm; aluminum, 3,000 ppm; magnesium, 3,000 ppm; sodium, 50 ppm; calcium, 200 ppm; titanium, 10 ppm; iron, 20 ppm; copper, 7 ppm; zinc, 5 ppm; silicon, 50 ppm; lead, 10 ppm; sulphur, 70 ppm; traces of zirconium, yttrium, gallium and boron. You can see from the above that there is absolutely nothing toxic in the burned or unburned mantles.

Finishing the report, I glanced up at the glowing mantle over my desk. It had been Welsbach's brilliant notion to cap a Bunsen burner with a fabric saturated in a chemical solution from which all organic matter could be burned off, leaving an incandescent metal ash. Some manufacturers hardened the mantles with heat-resistant beryllium, but the stuff proved toxic. Nevertheless, beryllium or no beryllium, the main mantle ingredient was 99 percent thorium—and it was then I discovered in my encyclopedia that thorium is radioactive.

Let me tell you about thorium. In 1828, a fellow named J. J. Berzelius gave the name to the oxide he had extracted from the rare mineral organite in Lovon, Norway. He named it after the highest deity of the heathen Scandinavians, Thor. Potent stuff. When heated, thorium ignites easily, burning with a bright white flame. It refuses to melt below about 1,750°C. Thorium is used in tungsten filaments for light bulbs and electronic tubes, welding rods, magnesium alloys, radiation therapy, and for the past hundred years, as the chief constituent in fuel lamp mantles.

Mantles are coated with a protective lacquer that you must burn off before using, preferably outdoors.

Perhaps you can guess my reaction to this news—had I inadvertently planted three radioactive devices smack-dab in the middle of my house? I was shocked, to put it mildly. What was a rural lamp keeper to do with this information?

Certainly, the measure of mantle safety cannot be taken optically. To understand lamp safety, I had to slip into the invisible dimension of radioactivity.

My first contact was with Wilmar Associates, where the Humphrey mantles had been tested.

"People are too damn worried!" announced W. S. Saese, when I asked about the potential for trouble from thorium. "The activity is so low you'd have to swallow 10 mantles to get an effect. The mantle is about as radioactive as television."

"Black and white or color?" I asked.

"Either."

Next I turned to science departments at Dartmouth College.

"I don't think you have anything to worry about," was the response I got from Roger Soderberg, professor of chemistry. "Maybe from particles, but the pressure is low and decay is extraordinarily slow. The half-life of thorium is extremely long. Gaslight is innocuous. It's been around 100 years and there have been no alarms."

Charles Drake, professor of earth sciences, agreed that thorium presented little threat. "The reason it's used is that it doesn't burn away, so nothing gets distributed. It's no more trouble than a rock sitting in a display cabinet."

At this point in my sleuthing I decided the mantle scare was a false alarm and dropped the matter. But a few years later *Mother Earth News* published an article called "The Hidden Danger of Lamp Mantles," by Mary Anderson. Her story reported on a class action suit against the Coleman Company and other mantle manufacturers. According to Anderson, a California health physicist named Walter Wagner had charged Coleman with endangering public health by using radioactive thorium in mantles. Specifically, Wagner sought to return $300 million in reputed damages to mantle purchasers and to require the company to begin using warning labels on their products.

Apparently, it was Wagner's contention that during thorium's decay, dangerous alpha and beta particles were emitted. The story painted a frightening picture: children, pregnant women, and unborn babies were at risk from "radium-laden fumes from lamp mantles" when a light was burning; and carrying a packaged mantle in a shirt or pants pocket exposed people to "significant" doses of beta radiation. "Users of mantle lamps should especially avoid breathing in the particulate ash or getting ash in their food," wrote the author.

Anderson confined her story essentially to a repetition of Wagner's allegations against the mantle manufacturers. However, *Mother Earth News* editors wrote an accompanying piece detailing some experiments they'd conducted with a small radiation detector. Indeed, they found that lamp mantles emitted anywhere from 0.05 to 0.30 millirems per hour, depending on whether they were in the package or on a lamp. But they felt compelled to add that low-level radiation of this sort is emitted by watches with radium-painted dials and certain kinds of crockery and pottery, which actually emit more radiation than lamp mantles. Other sources of low-level radiation are old clocks and timepieces, household smoke detectors, old kitchen timers, record and film static eliminators, concrete, brick, and in fact, rocks and soil—good old mother earth.

"Perhaps the main point of MOM's little test," the editors summed up, "is that it awakened us to the prevalence of sources of low-level radiation . . . . The big question, of course, is what dosage of low-level radiation places a human being at risk. This may never adequately be answered (and there may well be no 'safe' dosage)."

Nowhere was it mentioned that the U.S. Code of Federal Regulations classified thorium under the general heading "Unimportant quantities of source material" from naturally radioactive metallic elements, and exempts from all licensing "any quantities of thorium contained in (i) incandescent gas mantles, (ii) vacuum tubes, (iii) welding rods, (iv) electric lamps for illuminating purposes."

Despite those reassurances, there had been enough disturbing publicity and public concern about thorium mantles, to convince Coleman, Aladdin, and several other companies to eventually discontinue their use.

Ironically, many experienced lamp users were disappointed with the illuminating quality of the new yttrium mantle and continue to buy the thorium mantle from sources that still offer it.

And so I pass along one scientist's suggestions for the use and handling of thorium mantles.

• Mantles should not be handled by children, or pregnant or nursing women.

• The initial lighting should be done in a well-ventilated place.

• Mantles should never be placed in pockets.

• Users should avoid breathing the ash and avoid allowing the ash to contaminate food.

• Mantle lamps should never be burned without the chimney in place.

The Return
of Firelight

Over the past couple of decades there's been a revolution in wood and coal stove design; after decades of blackout, firelight is being restored to heating stoves. Crimson flames flicker behind glass door panes and stove-length windows, and the pages of magazine ads and brochures are ablaze. I'm looking at one ad now: a cozy couple snuggling up in front of their glazed firebox. NO COMMERCIAL INTERRUPTIONS, the headline crows. BRIGHT COLORS, MESMERIZING ACTION. Better than a Sony, indeed.

Over the centuries the trend in wood heat had been clear: the hearth warms up in inverse proportion to the light. Fireplaces waste heat—so close them up in a metal box. Mica and isinglass windows? Too fragile and not truly transparent. With the coming of the airtight stove, firelight was totally eclipsed.

Then the wood stove caught up with the space age. High-temperature, stress-resistant ceramic glass, developed for missile nose cones, drew the attention of the stove designers. By the late 1970s, responding to requests, Corning began to market a newly developed transparent stove glass called Pyroceram, and similar (and sometimes better) ceramic glasses started arriving from West Germany (notably Robax glass, made by Schott) and Japan (Nippon Electric Glass's Neoceram).

The Merits of Glass

The primary advantage of a fire-view is obvious: the window offers an instant reading of the condition of the fire, easing reloading— no damper and door to open to check the fire, no smoke spilling out into the house. And after dark the window doubles as a night-light.

Stovekeepers will recognize the practical merits of a fire gauge and night-light, but the Btu's that go with firelight may come as a surprise. While steel or iron stoves launch about 90 percent of their heat upward, a glass pane beams more outward. Glass doors affect the way radiation heat is transmitted. Pass your hand across the front of a glazed stove and feel the heat increase over the window; it's in the nature of glass to beat metal at transmitting heat. A pane of glass contains less mass than a similar one of steel or iron. Invisible electromagnetic waves in the infrared band of the spectrum also radiate from the flames and red coals, passing through the glass to heat on contact. Altogether, clear glass transmits up to 25 percent more heat than an equivalent expanse of metal.

Moreover, there's the psychological wave length. It's been proven that color perception can alter mood and biochemical reactions. Food looks brighter if you're hungry, and a dark room seems cold. But flood the scene with stovelight, and you might warm up your toes.

The fire-view stove appears to be a superior investment too. As one stove designer told me, "It's the fire-view that sells the stove." The stove buyer who foresees a resale or trade-in should consider one. At least that's what I thought when the time came for me to choose a wood stove for my new studio. Besides, I could use the extra candlepower.

Three Fire-View Stoves

So I began visiting stove dealers and writing letters to builders. What's the safest, warmest, brightest, glazed stove, I asked. I classified them into three types.

Franklin-type glass door stoves operate open or closed, both with a fire-view.

One type of stove is designed primarily for a fire-view. Usually it's a simple steel unit with a large window on the side. The glass is boxed into an offset frame something like a window box, full of flames instead of flowers. There's often a sill of about 6 inches between the glass and the stove wall opening. This type of stove is not airtight. The glass sits slightly loose in its molding, and supplementary vents draw air into the window box. This flow of air helps keep the glass cool and soot-free. Although these stoves are not technically airtight, they are still much more efficient than an open hearth. On some of these stoves the glass window can be closed off to tighten up the stove—but there goes the view. Stoves made from thin steel have problems of poor heat retention.

The second type of glazed stove is the airtight box stove—steel and/or iron—with glass in the front loading door. It generates higher temperatures than the vented window box stove and requires better thermal- and stress-resistant glass. Glazing an airtight firebox like this wasn't really feasible until recently. In fact, one designer had to use 9-inch Pyrex pie plates for windows. Pyrex was all right to a point—about 450°F. Beyond "broil," alas, the glass had a tendency to explode. Now the same stove maker uses "rocket" glass, heat resistant up to 2,000°F. One lingering problem with the fire-view box stove is that sometimes the logs are loaded from the front, and the door closes against the ends of the logs. As one designer wrote me, "occasionally breakage results when the glass, which is on the loading door, is used to push logs into the stove, or strikes a log that is too long for the stove." Sideloading stoves avoid that problem.

The third type of fire view is the airtight Franklin-type stove with glass in the fireplace doors. Ben Franklin had intended to combine the efficiency of the closed metal stove with the "healthful and cheering" effect of the flames. Trouble was, with the doors open the stove threw most of its heat up the chimney. It wasn't until stove makers put glass on the Franklin that you could have the views and heat both. Another advantage of the fireplace layout is that the logs lie parallel to the stove front, reducing chances of logs breaking the glass. Also, because the logs are viewed broadside, they yield more light. These stoves are usually cast iron, ceramic, or soapstone, with superior heat mass.

All things considered, it seemed to me that the airtight glazed Franklin offered the most. For unobstructed viewing, the stove could be run with doors wide open. To amplify heat and save fuel, the doors could be shut and the fire viewed through the glass. I knew that a slew of stove builders were producing the type, but my choice was easy. Not far north from where I live is the original home of Vermont Castings, pioneers in the design of fireplace stoves. At the time, they offered several models, all variations on one theme: highly baffled, cast iron airtights with swing-open viewing doors. The Defiant and the Vigilant, their earliest models, appeared with solid iron doors. Next was the Resolute: compact enough for my studio, and there in the front door was the window I wanted.

I drove up to Randolph for an afternoon of grilling the stove makers. I talked to people in customer service, design, and testing. Customer requests had persuaded the designers to try glass doors;

I learned that early Vermont Castings stoves incorporated a Japanese glass, which is clearer than Corning but occasionally crazes, covering over with a network of tiny cracks that blur the view. An ongoing problem with all of the glass-door stoves is carbon residue on the glass. For coal burners, this is not an issue; high temperature and low carbon content keep the glass clear. But wood burners had a gripe—foggy glass. Most stove manufacturers recommend running the stoves hot to avoid this problem.

Breakage turned out to be less trouble. After winnowing out some inferior views, the designers selected Robax, the ceramic pane made by Schott, a West German glassmaker. In addition to being heat-resistant, Robax (like the Nippon and Corning products) is strong enough to pass the stove industry impact standard: a 1-pound ball dropped on the glass from a couple of feet. I heard you could even throw snow on a hot window without cracking it. Besides having inherent resistance to impact and thermal shock, the Resolute stove glass is protected by an exterior iron grill.

In the testing shed I was escorted alongside a row of coal burning stoves. The windows were as bright as orange traffic lights. Then I spotted a stove with pitch-black glass. A wood burner.

"Is it always black?" I asked.

A stove tester opened the damper and added a scrap of dry lumber. The soot burned off like a rising curtain, releasing a flood of crimson. I was sold.

A blizzard blew in that night. By the time I had the stove ordered and a neighbor and his pickup corralled, 3 feet of snow covered the hills. We had to push the 300-pound stove crate up the road on a borrowed dogsled. My pal rode the sled back down, and I began to unpack. I followed the assembly instructions with a single exception. The glass is designed to be installed with an airtight gasket. I left it off, having received an unofficial tip that a loose window stays cleaner. Apparently the extra air circulation flushes away soot from the glass. I noticed that the window rattled a bit whenever I opened the fireplace door.

I situated the stove in the southwest corner of my studio, facing my desk, so that while I work, as I do now, I can look across the room into the fire. That first evening I watched the glass fill up with flames. Orange hues dappled the spruce walls. It was a whole new way to keep warm.

But after a couple of fires I thought the honeymoon might be over. Lighting the stove one morning, I saw that the window had smudged over. Perhaps it was that green maple I threw on? I loaded some bone-dry beech and kindled a wide-open fire. But I couldn't duplicate the disappearing act I'd seen in Randolph. Some carbon residues burned off, but a dark stain remained. It took a winter of dedicated pyromania to erase that smudge. What follows are the highlights of that stove study.

Grooming the Glass

First, I found that it was possible to regain clear glass using the window cleaner provided with the Resolute. (Newer stove designs create airflows that all but eliminate window soot.) I also found that I could also use a natural cleanser provided by your stove. Dampen a wad of newspaper, dip it in the ash bucket, and give the glass a polish. It works splendidly, and you can't beat the price.

It helps to crack the fireplace door a bit while waiting for the fire to catch on. That speeds up ignition and prevents smudging.

It's important to burn dry wood for a hotter fire with less accumulated carbon on the glass. Friends with coal stoves have encountered even fewer problems with smudging.

Don't add a lot of wood at once—it cools the fire down.

Run the stove with the damper open. This keeps the fire burning hot and allows residues to exhaust. It's less efficient, of course, and you won't do it all the time, but there's no getting around it: with the damper closed the glass is more likely to blacken.

Keep the chimney clean. The better the draft, the cleaner the glass. In fact, my hunch is that if I jumped from 6-inch to 8-inch stovepipe, the view would improve.

Eventually I installed the glass using the airtight gasket, and the stove actually burned more efficiently without affecting the view (and now the window doesn't rattle).

One day quite by chance I discovered my favorite glass-cleaning trick. I had just lit the stove. The glass was smudged black, and I didn't have time to rub it down with the cleaning solution. It happens that I had just cleaned my chain saw file with a wire brush. I picked up the brush and started to sweep the glass. The carbon stain peeled right off! I've heard that scraping can damage some stove glass, but on the Resolute it didn't leave a scratch. Steel wool also works.

Is all the elbow grease and extra wood worth it? I'm not sure you can measure firelight and come out in the black. But that's not the whole point. As a friend of mine said simply, "You do it for the glow."

STOVE GLASS

There are several types of heat-resistant glass suitable for stoves: tempered soda lime glass, tempered borosilicate glass, silica glass, and ceramic glass. Tempered soda lime glass is very clear but the least heat-resistant. It's suitable only for fireplaces or stoves with window vents. Should this type overheat and break, glass fragments may scatter explosively.

Tempered borosilicate glass, such as Corning's Pyrex, works at intermediate temperatures. This glass is used frequently in ovenware, panel heaters, and laboratory glassware. It will handle almost any thermal shock that may be encountered at operating temperatures below 450°F.

Silica glass, such as Corning's Vycor, is designed for ultra-high-temperature performance. It will handle any anticipated temperature and thermal shock requirements. It is suitable for both wood and coal burning stoves. Vycor is heavily rippled and not very clear.

Ceramic glass is composed of man-made materials. Its thermal properties are somewhat below ultra-high-temperature silica glass, but still suitable for most wood and coal stoves. One of its advantages is its low thermal expansion; it can be used over large expanses. And it can be remarkably clear, depending on the manufacturer. Corning's Pyroceram is tinted amber and looks out of focus; Nippon Electric Glass's Neoceram is sharper and untinted. Scott's Robax is the clearest.

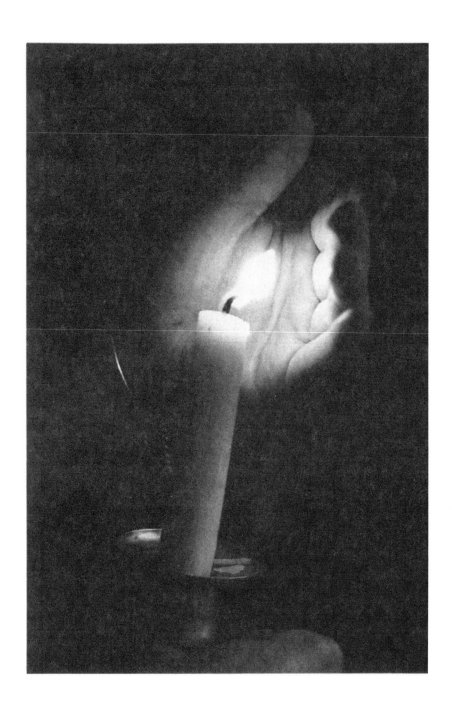

Sources

Candles

BatterySavers.com
c/o Sales Dept.
8125 Monetary Drive Suite H6
Riviera Beach, FL 33404
800-990-9110
www.batterysavers.com
Large supply of candles for everyday use and emergency preparedness.

Beeswax Candle Company
109 13th Street
Lynchburg, VA 24504
866-724-9300
www.beeswaxcandleco.com
Beeswax candles and accessories.

Blossomland Supply
311 West Front Street
Buchanan, MI 49107
269-695-2310
www.blossomland.com
Beeswax candle-making supplies, good how-to books, as well as beekeeping supplies.

Blue Corn Naturals
PO Box 122
31 South Glascow Avenue
Rico, CO 81332
970-967-2306
www.beeswaxcandles.com
Beeswax candles, beeswax, soywax, bulkwax, and miscellaneous candle-making products.

Candles and Supplies
500 Commerce Drive
Quakertown, PA 18951
215-538-8552
www.candlesandsupplies.com
Candle-making supplies, including waxes, molds, scents, wicks, and books.

Candlewic Company
3765 Old Easton Road
Doylestown, PA 18902
800-368-3352
www.candlewic.com
Candle-making supplies, including wax, molds, wicks, and books.

Honeycomb Hollow Candles
69 Route 28
West Harwich, MA 02671
877-430-7444
www.honeycombhollowcandles.com
Beeswax candles and accessories.

Lehman's
Mailing address: 289 Kurzen Road N., Dalton, OH 44618
Store address: 4779 Kidron Road, Kidron, OH 44636
888-438-5346
www.lehmans.com
Candles for everyday use and emergency lighting, and other lighting products. Excellent non-electric products catalog.

National Candle Association
1156 15th Street NW
Suite 900
Washington, DC 20005
202-393-2210
www.candles.org
National trade organization with an informative site and links.

Nitro-Pak Preparedness Center, Inc.
151 North Main Street
Heber City, UT 84032
800-866-4876
www.nitro-pak.com
Large supply of emergency preparedness candles for lighting and cooking.

Perin-Mowan, Inc.
4201 Barrett Drive
Hood River, OR 97031
541-386-3066
www.perinmowan.com
Beeswax candles.

Vermont Honeylights
9 Main Street
Bristol, VT 05443
800-322-2660
www.vermonthoneylights.com
Beeswax candles; also specializes in candles as artwork.

Fireview Stoves, Fireplaces, and Fireplace Inserts

Alaska Stove Company
3162 Columbia Boulevard
Bloomsburg, PA 17815
570-387-0260
www.alaskastove.com
Wood, coal, gas, and oil fire-view stoves.

Fireplace Products International (FPI)
988 Venture St.
Delta, British Columbia, Canada, V4G 1H4
604-946-5155
www.regency-fire.com
Regency and Hampton brand stoves.

Harman Stove Company
352 Mountain House Road
Halifax, PA 17032
www.harmanstoves.com
Coal, wood, pellet, corn, and gas fire-view stoves.

Hearth and Home Technologies
20802 Kensington Boulevard
Lakeville, MN 55044
800-669-4328
www.hearthnhome.com
Wood and gas fire-view stoves, and fireplace inserts.

Hearthstone
317 Stafford Ave.
Morrisville, VT 05661
802-888-5253
www.hearthstonestoves.com
Wood and gas fire-view stoves.

Jøtul
55 Hutcherson Drive
Gorham, ME 04039
800-797-5912
www.jotul.us
Wood and gas fire-view stoves and fireplace inserts, imported from Norway.

Lennox Hearth Products
1110 West Taft Avenue
Orange, CA 92865-4150
800-9-LENNOX
www.lennoxhearthproducts.com
Fire-view stoves, fireplaces, and fireplace inserts.

Morso
1011 Highway 52 West
Portland, TN 37148
615-323-0561
www.morsousa.com
Wood stoves and fireplace inserts.

The Thelin Company
12400 Loma Rica Drive
Grass Valley, CA 95945
800-949-5048
www.thelinco.com
Fireview wood, gas, and pellet burning stoves; features "state of the art" old-fashioned potbelly stove look.

Travis Industries
Mukilteo, Washington
www.travisindustries.com
Wood, gas, and pellet-burning stoves; fireplaces and inserts.

Vermont Castings
CFM Corporation
9695 Meadowdale Boulevard
Mississauga, Ontario, Canada, L5N 8A3
905-858-8010
www.vermontcastings.com
Wood and gas fueled fire-view stoves.

Wittus, Inc.
40 Westchester Avenue
Pound Ridge, NY 10576
914-764-5679
www.wittus.com
Imported German, UK, Dutch, Belgium, and Danish wood and gas
fire-view stoves and fireplaces.

Woodstock Soapstone Company, Inc.
66 Airport Road
West Lebanon, NH 03784
800-866-4344
www.woodstove.com
Wood and gas fire-view stoves.

Stove Information

www.oldhouseweb.com
Features useful information on various fire-view stoves, with links
to manufacturers.

www.fireplacesandwoodstoves.com
Useful information on various fire-view stoves and fireplaces.

www.hearth.com
Unbiased and independently run information source.

Lamps and Lanterns

www.aladdinknights.org
Informative site for Aladdin lamp owners and collectors.

Aladdin® Mantle Lamp Company
681 International Boulevard
Clarksville, TN 37040
800-457-5267
www.aladdinlamps.com
Aladdin® mantle lamps, chimneys, mantles, shades, brackets, wicks, and miscellaneous parts. Aladdin and Lox-on are registered trademarks of Aladdin Industries, LLC.

Cabela's
One Cabela Drive
Sidney, NE 69160
800-237-4444
www.cabelas.com
Excellent selection of lamps and lanterns from this prominent outdoor goods supplier.

Coleman Lamps, Inc.
PO Box 2931
Wichita, KS 67201-2931
800-835-3278
www.coleman.com
Liquid and pressurized fuel outdoor lamps, lanterns, and outdoor firelight torches.

Falks Lights
Galaxy Gas Products
1273 North Service Road East
Unit 5
Oakville, Ontario, Canada L6H 1A7
800-801-8512
info@galaxygas.com

Canadian-made indoor and outdoor LP or natural gas lights for cottages, hunting camps, off-the-grid living, and emergency preparedness. Sells primarily through dealers in the United States and Canada.

Humphrey Gaslights
24050 Commerce Park
Beachwood, OH 44122
216-360-9800
www.humphreygasproducts.com
Indoor LP and natural gas lights.

W. T. Kirkman
Ramona, CA 92065
877-985-5267
www.lanternet.com
Classy and classic kerosene lanterns from Dietz, Adlake, Handler, and other manufacturers. Also offers parts and many exclusive items, good information, and custom-made lighting equipment. They designed and built antique lanterns for Disneyland and Hollywood films, including *Pirates of the Caribbean* and *3:10 to Yuma.*

www.lampguild.org
Informative, non-commercial public formum for liquid fueled lighting research.

www.thelampworks.com
On-line resource for lighting researchers and collectors of oil and kerosene lamps.

Lehman's
Mailing address: 289 Kurzen Road N., Dalton, OH 44618
Store address: 4779 Kidron Road, Kidron, OH 44636
888-438-5346
www.lehmans.com
Comprehensive offering of fuel lamps and lanterns, and miscellaneous lighting equipment, from a variety of manufacturers.
Informative Web site and popular Ohio store for off-the-grid living; one of the best sources for alternative lighting information
and equipment. General catalogs and a special non-electric products catalog.

Midstate Lamp
169 East County Road
200 North
Arthus, IL 61911
866-450-5267
LP and natural gas indoor lighting.

Nitro-Pak Preparedness Center, Inc.
151 North Main Street
Heber City, UT 84032
800-866-4876
www.nitro-pak.com
A variety of non-electric lamps and lanterns from this well-stocked
emergency preparedness supplier.

Vermont Lanterns
54 Pleasant Street
Rutland, VT 05701
888-804-7404
www.y2klanterns.com
Large variety of kerosene lanterns for home, camping, boating,
and emergency use.

Gas Lighting Information

www.gasproductscompany.com

www.gas-lights.com

Index

Photograph page numbers are in **bold**.

The Earth Ponds Library

"Tim Matson is the guru of ponds." —*Albany Times-Union*

EARTH PONDS

The Country Pond Maker's Guide to Building, Maintenance, and Restoration
Tim Matson's classic guide, first published in 1982, remains the standard reference for pond owners and builders. Here is everything you need to know to plan, dig, sculpt, maintain, and enjoy your pond, and how to keep it healthy for years.
Paperback, ISBN 978-0-88150-155-1

EARTH PONDS A TO Z

An Illustrated Encyclopedia
This A–Z guide provides pond owners and builders with an at-a-glance reference to answer any question. From Acid Rain to Zooplankton, pond guru Tim Matson defines and explains more than 200 terms associated with pond building and maintenance. Here you'll find descriptions and definitions of all significant pond elements, including structural features, construction materials, aquacultural topics and crops, environmental concerns, government support and regulating agencies, and more.
Paperback, ISBN 978-0-88150-494-1

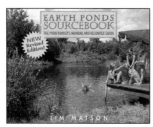

EARTH PONDS SOURCEBOOK

The Pond Owner's Manual and Resource Guide
As the popularity of ponds continues to grow, pond design, construction and maintenance, products, and the information expand as well. This is the most comprehensive and up-to-date reference for pond-related books and periodicals; aquaculture manufacturers and suppliers; advocacy groups and organizations; water gardening suppliers, botanical gardeners, and government organizations.
Paperback, ISBN 978-0-88150-612-9

Available through The Countryman Press and wherever books are sold.
To order, call **1-800-245-4151** or visit **www.countrymanpress.com**.

For more information about The Earth Ponds Company,
visit Tim Matson's Web site at **www.earthponds.com**.